*Praise for*

# SPIRITUAL PREPPER

In this challenging and sobering book, Jake exposes the Christian subculture in twenty-first-century America to biblical and contemporary reality. He lovingly removes dangerous illusions, which have collectively become a seemingly inescapable hindrance to genuine spiritual growth for many Christians in America today. Jake reminds Christians that we are pilgrims on a difficult but right road, making the journey towards a better country and a reward incomparable. Every Christian who sometimes (or regularly) confuses the American Dream with true spiritual success will benefit from reading this helpful and practical resource.

—MARC MINTER, LEAD PASTOR FIRST BAPTIST CHURCH
   OF DIANA, TEXAS, AND TEAM IMPACT TEAM LEADER

I love Jake's fearless, hot heart for God. In *Spiritual Prepper,* you won't find courage with any swagger whatsoever. On the contrary, you will be humbly encouraged to stand up to whatever the world and the devil's dark forces throw at you.

—DR MARK DANCE, LIFEWAY PASTORS

Jake McCandless raised the hammer, aimed at his target, and adeptly drove the nail firmly into place. Salted with true stories that quickly pull you along a journey of sound biblical instruction and perspective, the author leads you to the heart of faithful Christian living in the midst of our profoundly prophetic times.

—CARL GALLUPS PASTOR AND AUTHOR OF FIVE BOOKS
INCLUDING *WHEN THE LION ROARS*

In an age of moral and spiritual decline, Christians face dangers from every direction. Sometimes the biggest danger is their denial or lack of awareness of the challenges that surround them. As church attendance declines and large portions of the millennial generation fall away from faith, it can be tempting to give in to discouragement or despair. However, in *Spiritual Prepper* Jake McCandless offers reasons for hope. Faith does not *have* to fade. Just as doomsday preppers make checklists of supplies for physical survival, this book offers checklists for spiritual survival. McCandless shows readers how to get ready to survive and overcome persecution, trials, temptations, false teaching, and other spiritual crises. His prophetic and loving voice is exactly the wake-up call the church needs today.

—JOSEPH BENTZ, AUTHOR OF *NOTHING IS WASTED*

*Spiritual Prepper* is a call to action for pastors, parents, professors, and everyone else who claims to know Christ as Savior. This book may disturb you; It will absolutely challenge you; but most of all it will compel you to answer one crucial question: Have you adequately "prepped" your children, grandchildren, students, and friends for the impending spiritual doomsday? If you believe the truth of God's inerrant word, you cannot ignore that question. Read this book—and get ready for battle.

—TERRY KIMBROW, PRESIDENT, CENTRAL BAPTIST COLLEGE, CONWAY, ARKANSAS

I've known Jake for many years, and his wisdom has always surpassed his years. That fact is very evident in *Spiritual Prepper*. Prophecy can be a scary dive into the deep unknown for many people, and that's why I believe many choose to steer clear of the topic. However, Jake has done an amazing job of making prophecy understandable and relatable to every day life, but at the same time keeping the focus on having a steadfast, unshakable relationship with Christ. This book is a great read for everyone, from being an encouragement to new Christians to being an excellent refresher course for those more seasoned in their faith. I believe I'll be rereading this one for years to come.

—KEN REED, SEVENTH DAY SLUMBER

# Spiritual
## PREPPER

# Spiritual
# PREPPER

TAPPING INTO OVERLOOKED PROPHECIES TO PREPARE YOU FOR DOOMSDAY

## JAKE MCCANDLESS

 WND Books

# *Spiritual* PREPPER

Published by WND Books, Washington, D.C. WND Books is a registered trademark of WorldNetDaily.com, Inc. ("WND")

Book designed by Mark Karis

All the stories in this book are true. Although, the names and places have been changed to protect the identity of the people involved.

WND Books are available at special discounts for bulk purchases. WND Books also publishes books in electronic formats. For more information call (541) 474-1776, e-mail orders@wndbooks.com, or visit www.wndbooks.com.

Paperback ISBN: 978-1-944229-54-2
eBook ISBN: 978-1-944229-55-9

Library of Congress Cataloging-in-Publication Data

*Printed in the United States of America*
17 18 19 20 21 LBM 9 8 7 6 5 4 3 2 1

*With my wife, Amanda, we dedicate this book and its ministry to our daughters, Andrea and Addison.*

*The support and sacrifice of your mom and my work is in the hope you would trust Jesus and follow Him all the days of your life.*

# Contents

# *Foreword*

DON'T YOU LOVE THE COVER OF THIS BOOK?

Surprisingly, the overriding question in biblical prophecy isn't how the *world* is going to end. Instead, the big question is: How are *you* going to finish?

Wiped out? Or a survivor?

After all, "Silently and imperceptibly as we work or sleep, we grow strong or we grow weak," B. F. Westcott reminds us. So, how do we know which?

Author Jake McCandless aptly calls it a spiritual disaster.

I only wish I had read *Spiritual Prepper: Tapping into Overlooked Prophecies to Prepare You for Doomsday* before my own spiritual disaster.

My love for God, joy for life, and peace were shattered. In their place I felt angry, deceived, and desperate for a way out of my nightmare. In my despair, I doubted God's character. Finally, the day came I couldn't read the Bible anymore. Not a single verse. I couldn't pray, even over a meal. For days and weeks on end.

Experientially, I had lost my faith. Why? Because I had failed to heed the clear warnings of Scripture. And because I'd let the circumstances of life temporarily overshadow what I *knew* to be true. As a result, I couldn't fall asleep at night. I couldn't get rid of the stabbing pain in my chest. I was *this* close to my own spiritual doomsday.

Thankfully, God renewed my faith when I forced myself to open my Bible, read a verse, and honestly answer the question, "Do I believe it?" To my surprise, I said "yes." It wasn't a big "yes!" But it was enough to prompt me to read another verse, and then another. In time, God gave me a much stronger and more robust faith. Thanks to Him, and Him alone, a full-scale spiritual doomsday was narrowly averted.

Since then, I've talked with many other people about my experience. Even crazy places like UC Berkeley. Not because my story is dramatic, but because it's true to life. *Every* Christian is seriously tempted, at one time or another, to lose his or her faith. If only I hadn't overlooked some of the Bible's most important prophecies.

Don't wait until the day of crisis. Instead, push everything else aside and read this book cover to cover. Take its message seriously. And, above all, don't put it back on a shelf. Instead, share it with your friends!

—DAVID SANFORD, SPEAKER AND AUTHOR OF *LOVING YOUR NEIGHBOR: SURPRISE! IT'S NOT WHAT YOU THINK*

# *Acknowledgments*

SOME PEOPLE SAY IT TAKES A VILLAGE to raise a child, well, it took a *nation* to turn me into an author. No one has done more than my wife, Amanda, who has always let me draw "ligers" with only the minimum of complaining. She gave up her only weekly break to allow me to write. Thank you for being so supportive and for taking care of reality, so I could live with my heads in the clouds.

Next are my daughters, Andrea and Addison. I hope one day they will understand there was a purpose to Dad's typing away with his headphones listening to "apple" music. Girls, thank you for being so proud of your Dad and for praying for angels (agents) and pooters (publishers) to like Daddy's book.

Thank you, Mom and Dad for sacrificing your own wants to allow me to feel like I could do anything. Thank you for the endless support, and enduring a son who has been in mad-scientist mode. A big thank you to my mother-in-law and father-in-law for literally opening your doors to show your support and enthusiasm. Thank you Kylie and Jesse for your enduring hearing about this deal over and over. I have been blessed with the greatest grandparents in the world who laid a godly heritage in my family. Thank you for your support. I also thank my extended family for their support, and especially Linda for watching the girls.

There've been so many friends that genuinely encouraged me with their interest, long with those who have pushed me to write over the years—thank you. I know you wondered if the end times would come before this book was finished. Justin, thanks for being a catalyst for God to get a hold of me on this subject. Speaking of family and friends, a big thank you is in order for my church family at Mount Vernon Baptist Church. You all cheered for me and allowed me to serve while writing. David, thanks for picking up the slack and getting me out of the office. Karen and Carey, thank you for running everything while I wrote.

A big thank you to my agent, Cyle Young. Thanks for believing in writers and especially me. I hope this book buys you more than a cup of coffee. Hartline Literary Agency, thank you for believing in Cyle so he could believe in me.

Thank you, WND Team, for giving me this opportunity. I feel so blessed to be a part of a publishing and culture-changing team that is fighting the good fight. Geoff, thank you for your patience with me.

There are so many who have helped me on the writing end, but none more than my writing team—Rita, Liz, and Ryan. Thank you for your time and holding me to the fire. Rita, thank you for emptying many ink pens on my manuscript. I also thank my BRMCWC family. Along with the A3 team, you guys have been such "holy introducers." I especially thank Joseph Bentz who made me feel I could do this writing thing. Also Blythe Daniels, your guidance was right on. Alycia Morales, thank you for your help on my proposal.

This has been a team effort, thank you for believing in me and this message.

# Introduction

THERE ARE PROPHECIES YOU'VE NOT BEEN TOLD.

Prophecies that have been overlooked.

Prophecies that have been overshadowed by those that are more sensational and make better movies.

Prophecies that haven't been taught as they should but that you need to know.

Prophecies that apply, more than any others, to your everyday life.

Prophecies that explain the reasons for the current struggles Christians encounter around the world. These prophecies shed light on

why our brothers and sisters are being killed for their faith

why Christian children are being sold into slavery and their parents remain behind bars why our nation is slipping into deep immorality—and the church isn't doing much better

why our nation is disposing of our religious liberties

why our churches in America are empty and millions of professing Christians no longer attend

why our churches are losing their young people at unfathomable rates

why we struggle with complacency and sin ourselves

why we might turn from our faith

Not only do these prophetic passages help us understand and cope with the challenges of the faith today, but more important, they warn us of what might possibly be our own spiritual doomsday.

By knowing these forgotten prophecies, we can understand that God is still in control and that we're still on the winning side, even when the world is telling us differently. By coming to terms with the truth, we can know what we need to do to prepare ourselves for a turbulent future.

I believe you hope, as I do, to hear upon seeing Jesus, "Well done, My good and faithful servant." If that's not your desire now, it *will* be when you cross over into eternity.

You can hear those words. You are equipped and empowered to remain faithful in the midst of the greatest of challenges to your faith. The struggle is that your path ahead is full of spiritual disasters. We need to identify those disasters, and forgotten prophecies revealed in this book are the key. They will guide us through this challenging gauntlet of life.

This prophecy book is unlike most, as the prophecies I address focus on our spirituality, morality, and faith, not the environment, economy, or geopolitics.

The heart of this book is to bring awareness to the dangers that threaten our faith. Real dangers that pose a grave threat, but I want to help you begin to spiritually prepare for this adversity. One of the trademark features in resources for doomsday preppers are checklists. Following these lists ensure survivalists they have all they need to survive. Even if you're simply headed into a storm shelter it helps to have a list of what you need to ride out the storm—weather radio, batteries, water, blankets, food, etc.

Since we've accepted the challenge to prep to remain faithful with the intensity of a physical doomsday prepper, we also need a checklist—a spiritual prepper checklist. At the end of each chapter I've included a checklist of how to prepare spiritually. A master checklist is presented in the final chapter.

Will you journey with me to examine these forgotten prophecies and the warnings they give us? I pray you will so that you may begin *prepping for our spiritual doomsday.*

First, let's look at some terminology you will see throughout the book.

DEFINITIONS

**spiritual disaster**: an event that occurs in the life of a follower of Christ that challenges his or her faith and the practice of it. Just as physical disasters, such as hurricanes, tornados, floods, earthquakes, and war have the potential of destroying our physical life, a spiritual disaster has the potential to wreck our faith and our practice of it.

**spiritual doomsday: 1:** any event and its aftermath that follows a Christian's failure to remain faithful when faced with a spiritual disaster, and his or her subsequent turning away from faith; **2:** the final wave of spiritual disasters Christians will face at the end of the current age.

**turn away:** to depart. The focal Bible passage of this book is Matthew 24:10. In this passage we're told that due to the certain spiritual disasters described throughout that chapter, many will "turn away" from the faith. The Greek word translated "turn away" or "fall away" is σκανδαλίζω, which means "to cause one to stumble." I will provide more insight on this phrase as it is used to describe Peter's denial and the scattering of the disciples following Jesus' arrest in Matthew 26:31. At a minimum, the term applies to a lapse, whether temporary or long term, in the practice of one's faith.

# 1

## PREPPING FOR PROPHETIC FULFILLMENT

"Do not be afraid of those who kill the body but cannot kill the soul. Rather, be afraid of the One who can destroy both soul and body in hell."

—MATTHEW 10:28

### THE QUESTION

Sabir helplessly watched as three Islamic State soldiers with spray paint cans painted a red symbol on his front gate. The symbol was familiar to Sabir's family—used daily—it was one of the letters of their alphabet. But the mark itself meant so much more.

The soldiers had painted an Arabic N, or ن. It stands for Nazarene. The symbol identified Sabir and his family as

Christians—followers of Jesus the Nazarene.

Their home wasn't the only one in their city to receive this mark. Sabir's family had heard reports from other cities, and those homes were not only marked, but were raided. The homeowners were then questioned, and the fate of their families rested upon how those questions were answered.

Thank goodness that didn't happen here.

Months passed; the paint on the gate had faded, though it still remained. Islamic State occupation continued, and their squeeze on everyday life tightened. But the family's fear had subsided with the passage of time, and they'd almost forgotten about the painted mark.

Their fear was about to return.

A forceful cadence of knocks on the front door interrupted the family dinner one evening. Praying a silent short prayer, Sabir walked to the door as his wife, Kalila, rushed the children and her parents into a back room. Her frail father frantically prayed over the huddled family.

Sabir opened the door and found himself face-to-face with not three, but five masked Islamic States soldiers. And this time they carried rifles, not spray paint.

That was when *it* came—the *question*.

The *question* on which the family's fate rested.

The father of four knew what the soldiers were looking to hear. There was one answer that would allow his family to remain in their home. The answer, at a minimum, would keep them from not paying a hefty tax and at most would keep them alive.

For years this scenario had run through his head, making the *question* all too familiar. A single answer could save his family's lives. So much hung in the balance with his answer.

But his decision on how to answer wasn't that simple—for something beyond physical survival hung in the balance. Something that because of its very nature could not be quantified. That something was *eternity*.

It was for *eternity*. It was for *heaven*. It was for the *glory of God*. It was for their *souls*—not their physical lives—that Sabir answered the question. With an emphatic boldness and an uncanny strength, he proclaimed to the soldiers, "Yes, I am a Christian. I follow the Nazarene.

Immediately the soldiers pounced on him, beating him with the butts of their rifles. Then their fists. Even after he fell, they continued beating him.

One soldier continued the beating while the other four raided the house. They rushed into the back room where the rest of the family was huddled and praying. Two soldiers grabbed Kalila, prying her from her children, and they dragged her into the living room and threw her on the sofa. Then one of the soldiers began, in the sight of everyone, doing unthinkable things to her. Her husband lay barely breathing in a pool of his own blood outside the front door.

Two of the soldiers grabbed the two daughters, Nathifa and Nawal. The ISIS fighters were happy—these girls would bring a large price on the slave market since they were only eight and nine years old. They were led out to a waiting truck. Leading the youngest son out the door, the soldier told the dying father, "This boy will be taught to kill infidels like you."

The three youngest children had been loaded up—the girls to be sold and abused and the boy to be brainwashed and trained to fight. Meanwhile, another soldier had taken a turn with Kalila. She tried not to scream because Sabir could hear.

She wouldn't cause him any more pain.

Hana, the oldest son, at fifteen, was dragged to the middle of the adjacent street and ordered onto his knees. Then the soldiers dragged Sabir next to him. Two soldiers simultaneously put a .45-caliber bullet into the backs of Hana's and Sabir's heads; then they removed their heads with knives. The bodies and heads were left beneath the spray-painted mark on the family's gate.

After a third soldier's attack, Kalila was carried to a second truck, separate from the children. One soldier said she might bring forty-five dollars, but even that wouldn't be worth it.

Kalila's aging parents had been left for the moment but knew ISIS would be back. When the soldiers returned, the only way they could remain in their home would be if they paid the *jizya*, a tax paid in covenant for the protection of ISIS. They needed to make their way to one of the refugee camps, but weren't sure they could even physically make it.

When the dust cleared, Sabir's and his oldest son's beheaded bodies lay next to the street. Sabir's wife had been raped multiple times and was now carried away to be sold into slavery. His two daughters would be sold as sex slaves. His youngest son was on his way to a makeshift prison to be brainwashed to become an ISIS soldier. His in-laws were left in the mess, and now would have to take a long trek through the desert to find refuge.

The carnage seemed to prove that Sabir had answered the soldier's question wrong, but time will tell that Sabir's answer was *best*. Although it looks as though he lost, he actually had successfully survived a spiritual disaster and kept himself from a failure of faith—a spiritual doomsday.

## THE RIGHT ANSWER

You might say, "Sabir gave the *right answer*? How could that be? There is no way that could be the case."

Don't risk those babies, right?

Save yourself. Live to fight another day.

THINK ABOUT YOUR CHILDREN!

How could Sabir have done the right thing when *he* caused himself and his son to be killed and beheaded, his wife to be raped, his daughters to be sold into slavery, and his youngest son to be kidnapped? How could that be the best way?

How *he* answered the question caused all the trouble.

If only *he* had given the answer the soldiers wanted to hear.

If only he'd denied Christ. If only he'd hidden his faith— maybe even just lied.

If only—then his family would be alive. Safe and sound in their home.

What would make someone make such a decision?

At an absolute unfathomable cost, Sabir kept his faith and remained faithful.

How would *I have* answered *the question* with my children in the back room? How would *you*?

I realize that answering as Sabir did and bringing such a fate upon him and his family sounds absolutely ridiculous. They could have just told a little white lie and covered their tracks. The family could have kept their faith internal, knowing they had a personal relationship with Christ and that mattered the most. Christianity is about a relationship, so why would it matter how they practiced that faith? They could have stayed alive and God could have used them some more, right? That all sounds logical and makes sense to me. What about you?

So what would cause a man to boldly proclaim to belong to Christ when hell was about to rain down on him?

It was faith. Obedience. His love for Christ. And believe it or not—his love for his family.

No doubt, scriptures were ringing in Sabir's head:

"Whoever acknowledges me before others, I will also acknowledge before my Father in heaven. But whoever disowns me before others, I will disown before my Father in heaven." (Matt. 10:32–33)

"Do not be afraid of those who kill the body but cannot kill the soul." (Matt. 10:28)

"Be faithful even to the point of death, and I will give you life." (Rev. 2:10)

"But the one who stands firm to the end will be saved." (Matt. 24:13)

Biblical examples of others who had stood faithfully against the odds also may have run through Sabir's mind, like the stories of Stephen, who was stoned to death for proclaiming Christ—and saw heaven (Acts 7); Daniel, who continued to pray to his God, even though he would be thrown into a lion's den (Dan. 6); and Shadrach, Meshach, and Abednego, who were thrown into a blazing furnace because they refused to turn from their faith (Dan. 3).

Sabir had this instruction from Scripture written in his heart. He understood that God desires faithfulness and obedience. Sabir and Kalila had a great confidence in God, taking Him at His Word. They knew God would take care of them, and even trusted that following His commands was the best for their family. Even if their children faced physical harm, it would be worth the price paid because the age to come far outweighed this life. Knowing the passages that helped guide Sabir should help us make sense of how someone could offer his life in service to God.

In talking with families whose children serve as missionaries in dangerous lands, I've learned that it's a great struggle for them knowing their sons and daughters might face persecution. It's extremely hard to understand why someone would risk his or her life, especially when it's someone we know and love, and even more so when the threat involves one of our own children.

Yet, somehow God is more glorified in martyrdom than in anything else. This must be because the refusal to recant your faith, while knowing your life and the lives of the ones you love will end, boldly states to the world that your faith, your God, and eternity far outweigh this world in importance. It's in that stance that God receives glory.

This story of Sabir and his family, though fictional, is based on factual reports of what Christians and other ethnic groups are presently facing in Iraq and Syria. In a recent book, *Defying Isis,* humanitarian Johnnie Moore shares true accounts of the persecution of Christians at the hands of ISIS, stories he learned firsthand through his work helping displaced Christians and other religious minorities in Iraq and Syria.

One such story involves an Iraqi pastor who had received word that ISIS was coming to his village. The pastor traveled hurriedly from house to house, warning his congregation and urging them to escape. Eventually, though, time ran out for his beloved Christian brothers and sisters. He knew the families who remained wouldn't have time to get out of the country. At one of these homes he stuck his head in the doorway and gave them "coy advice," saying, "When ISIS arrives they'll come to your door and they'll ask you if you're Christian or Muslim. I'd tell them 'I am a follower of Jesus.'" He continued, "If you choose to not convert, then just know it will only hurt for a second. I'm praying for you."[1] The four members of that family didn't convert and were martyred.

How does a pastor boldly offer such advice—especially knowing that advice would bring death to a family? The pastor's confidence in God allowed this. His confidence is a confidence that I believe you also have, or desire to have.

I know I desire to have such a faith, and to stand with faith as the heroes before us have done. I desire to be faithful even while staring down the barrel of a gun, and to be obedient even when the lives of my family are on the line. I believe you feel the same way. Although that is the deepest desire of my heart, it'd be extremely hard to make that decision. I struggle to know that I could stand as Sabir did. You may struggle as well.

I don't think we are alone—I imagine even the boldest of God's people who have offered their lives up as martyrs have struggled. But in the end they were able to remain faithful and to overcome. We, too, can overcome. We possess the same power through the Holy Spirit that they did. The same Spirit who strengthened Stephen before the Sanhedrin, Peter before the Roman executioners, and Polycarp at the stake empowers us to be "more than conquerors" (see Rom. 8:37). We've been empowered to overcome persecution, or any other spiritual disaster.

We can be faithful like Sabir.

## NO SURPRISE

The story describing what Christians are facing in the Middle East today is a punch in the gut.

The account is horrific. It's evil.

But it isn't surprising. Not at all.

We shouldn't be shocked.

The news reports of the persecution of our brothers and sisters in Christ makes my blood boil and fills me with compassion for the martyrs, but I'm not surprised. I expect it. We all should. The only surprising news is that there are nations where Christians aren't being persecuted.

Jesus Himself said that persecution would happen. He foretold it in Scripture. One such passage is Matthew 24:9–10: "Then you will be handed over to be persecuted and put to death, and you will be hated by all nations because of me. At that time many will turn away from the faith and will betray and hate each other."

You're probably familiar with that passage, but you may have never thought that it applied to *your* everyday life. In general, when we think of prophecy, we think of topics such as Jesus' return, the rise of the Antichrist, economic difficulties, or astonishing signs in the heavens. We tend to focus on the sensational images in prophecy. Most of the attention in prophetic studies has been given to the political, economic, or environmental aspects of the future. Yet, even as prophecy warns of what will happen in the world physically, it also foretells what will happen spiritually. There are many passages along these lines.

We're told in Luke that the last days will be morally bankrupt, like the world during Noah's time and in Lot's time (see 17:27–30). According to the apostle Paul, people will become lovers of themselves (2 Tim. 3:1–5). Those are just a couple of examples. It's the prophecies of moral and spiritual decline that have been forgotten, or at least overshadowed. At a minimum these passages haven't been treated or presented as prophecies. This is a great shame because events concerning the spiritual realm are what we should fear the most.

Matthew 24 is clearly understood as prophecy. It is used often to explain the physical events that will occur at the end of the age, which is an accurate interpretation. Persecution is always on that list. So the prophecy itself isn't forgotten, but the spiritual aspect is. The most important part of this portion of Scripture is the prediction that due to these physical events, many followers of Christ will turn away from their faith and quit practicing it. This is a warning to us.

Most readers consider the prophecies in Matthew 24 to refer exclusively to the end of the age, but they weren't intended to only be descriptions of the end. At the end of the age preceding Jesus' return, the events listed in that chapter will become universal and reach their maximum intensity. They include the challenges to the faith of believers from the time Jesus ascended into heaven until He returns. Therefore, these overshadowed prophecies are vital to our everyday life. Every Christian in history and in the future will encounter these trials.

The prophecy in Matthew 24:9–10, written two thousand years ago, explains the persecution of the early church at the hands of the Romans. It also explains the Armenian Genocide in 1915, when 1.5 million Armenian Christians were killed. But even more amazing, this same prophecy explains what's happening in the Middle East, northern Africa, and North Korea *today*. These forgotten prophecies are important in helping us make sense of the events occurring in our world—events in which it feels that God has lost control.

He hasn't. He knew these things would happen long before they did. And the current chaos hasn't changed the fact that in the end, He'll win.

Maybe even more important than this passage's explanation of current events is that it gives a somber warning of a possible future spiritual doomsday. This prophecy foretold that when followers of Christ run into persecution, "many will turn away" (v. 10). They will deny Christ or, at least, quit actively practicing the faith. Sabir faced this possibility. His persecution could have been a challenge that squelched his faith, but he remained faithful.

## OUR TURN

ISIS' warpath in Syria and Iraq, with its terrifying images, isn't the only trying news that scrolls across my home page. Each time I view the news here in the United States, my heart breaks. My heart is further crushed and stirred when I visit and counsel those who have been personally impacted and hurt by the declining moral climate of America and a weakened American church.

The forgotten and overshadowed prophecies shed light on the current moral climate in America. And again, as with persecution around the world, we shouldn't be surprised. Trusted statisticians, researchers, and church leaders have documented the dismal shape of the American church and the immoral condition of the nation. One of the most vivid description of America's present moral states is found in Steve Hale's 2006 book, *Truth Decay,* in which he compares America to a sinking ship like the *Titanic.* "Our ship is taking on water," he wrote.[2]

Although the discouraging descriptions can be backed by statistics, I don't imagine they're necessary to convince you of the depths of the immorality that permeates our nation. You see and live it every day while you fight to remain faithful in the midst of it. Today we are witness to, not only complacency in the church, but an overall moral decline in our nation. Matthew 24:12 foretold of this "increase of wickedness." It shouldn't be surprising that there have been attempts to redefine marriage, and that whole denominations now accept behavior that has been considered sinful throughout the entire two-thousand-year history of Christianity. Prophecies such as these will help us come to terms with how our nation could dispose of religious liberties so easily.

If we pay attention to these prophecies, we will understand why many churches are empty and why the church at large is losing so many young people. Lifeway president and researcher, Thom Rainer, wrote that 70 percent of children and teens raised in church will leave by the age of twenty-two.[3] At the current astonishing rate, we can expect denominations to shrink in size and baptisms to drop off dramatically. Recent headlines forewarn the grim news, indicating that the Southern Baptist Convention, which appears to be faring better than other denominations, saw the biggest decline in membership since 1881.[4]

In 2008, based on detailed analysis published by the U.S. Census Bureau and the Barna Group, it was reported by David Sanford, author of *If God Disappears*, that there were 31 million professed Christians in the United States who had quit attending church.[5] He conveyed to me the seriousness of the situation: "Any business that is losing 31 million customers is going out of business,"[6] In a later blog post in 2015, Sanford updated that the number of Christians who had left the church had risen to 42 million.[7]

This statistic is mind-boggling, so much so that news organizations have actually refused to publish articles I submitted because they thought the numbers were too high.

In a 2013 study, Pew Research concluded that only 37 percent of all Americans were regular church attenders.[8] When looking at just the number of Christians, according to the 2010 US census, 109 million American Christians are not regular church attenders, or only 44 percent of professing Christians. The Barna Group concluded that only 41 percent of professed Christians were not attending church.[9] This may look like a bad situation for the church, but it is one that is not contrary to overlooked prophecies in our Bibles.

Returning to the issue of the many who once attended and now quit, in a study released by the Francis A. Schaeffer Institute of Church Leadership Development it was found that presently 2.7 million church members fall into inactivity a year.[10] The *Christian Post* presented a number half that size, but still saw this even as epidemic with 3,500 individuals leaving the church each day.[11]

Along with causing many to abandon the living out of their faith these spiritual disasters have caused moral transformation and devastation to families and the church in America.

Along with describing these other events, the forgotten prophecies of Scripture should remind us that these spiritual disasters could even cause us to stumble, just as the apostle Peter did when he denied Christ three times. (See Matt. 26:69–75; Mark 14:66–72; et al.) Even being as strong as Peter, we can easily become part of the millions.

Just as Sabir faced a pivotal moment in his faith, we do too. Sabir overcame his fear, doubt, and temptation to deny Christ. We can too.

## PREPARED

I chose a story of persecution unto death of a man and his children as my illustration because I don't believe there is a greater threat to our faithfulness than the prospect of harm to our own children. But if someone like Sabir could face this trial and still remain faithful—and many have—then we could remain faithful too. Even though the spiritual disaster we face may be very different, the same consequences are at stake. Such faithfulness on our part requires the same confidence in God and His Word.

And yet, many of those whose faith has failed in difficult times had great confidence in God. So there must be something else that one must add to his or her faith to survive a possible spiritual doomsday.

That something else is "prepping."

As I write this, the two rivers on each side of my hometown are swollen well beyond the major flood stage. They're both approaching record levels.

My hometown is far downstream. When tons of rain fell upriver and those upper lakes began to spill over their dams, officials issued flood warnings. After hearing those reports residents sprang into action. They evacuated homes. They led their livestock to higher ground. They built levees. The residents heeded the warnings. They recognized the events that were occurring, and they prepared accordingly. Because they *prepared*, they will survive, and so will their property.

Sabir and his family were prepared. The family had been warned of the threat ISIS posed. Going a step further, they recognized that persecution was taking place, and they knew it could also affect them. They had studied the warnings from Scripture not to deny Jesus. They had also "prepped." Sabir and Kalila had considered the possibilities, and had discussed them at length. Even knowing what would happen to their children, they decided that remaining faithful to the Lord was more critical than what might happen to their children. They assured one another that they wanted faithfulness even over life. Our faithfulness is just as important in the challenges we face.

Doomsday preppers go to great lengths creating bunkers, storing water and food, acquiring ammunition, and receiving training to survive whatever they may face. They strategize based on speculation on world events and how they might be affected. If they do all of this just to preserve their fragile, temporary lives, shouldn't we prep for the certainty of a spiritual doomsday, as Scripture foretells?

# SPIRITUAL PREPPER'S CHECKLIST

As you prepare for prophetic fulfillment, it is important to be aware of what the Bible says about the last days so you can know what to expect. Here in chapter 1, I leave you with three items.

☐ Recognize there will be challenges to your faith.

This may sound simple, but many American Christians believe that a faith-filled life means there won't be any difficulty. It is vital to come to terms with the biblical reality that trials will come and to study Scripture—especially prophecy—so that you'll know the challenges that lie ahead.

First, create a counterculture mind-set that fully comprehends the Christian walk is one challenge after another; it's not a bed of roses. Yet at the same time we can completely trust God is going to take care of us and the reward for faithfulness far exceeds anything we might gain on this earth.

To have a correct mind-set of a Christian journey full of trials we need to study the whole counsel of Scripture. If you haven't had a concentrated time in your life where you intentionally studied God's Word as you did other subjects in school, now is the time. Join a local Bible study, enroll in classes at church or a Bible college, or take classes online. Such training and study is not only for ministers but for all followers of Christ. If you have taken formal classes in the past, keep up your individual and corporate studies in a Sunday school class, Bible study, or small group, and use study tools such as Bible dictionaries, handbooks, and commentaries to help you in your studies.

☐ Resolve to remain faithful no matter what you face.

Before you face great difficulty, make the decision to remain faithful, and not to deny Christ regardless of what you might encounter. Plan ahead. You have a greater chance of standing strong if you have made that commitment before you are in the heat of the moment. Write down your resolution and share it with others.

☐ Openly discuss the dangers to your faith with family and church.

As mentioned earlier Sabir and Kalila were prepared to make a decision to profess Christ even at the expense of their children because they had an open discussion of the issue. In the Bible we read of the dangers the early church faced, and today there are reports of persecution to Christians in underground churches around the world. In America, we tend to sweep those possibilities under the rug. It is important that you talk openly about possible spiritual disasters with those you love. It also needs to be spoken openly and boldly in your church, small group meetings, and Sunday school classes.

# 2

# PREPPING TO BE FAITHFUL

I give you this instruction in keeping with the prophecies once made about you, so that by following them you may fight the good fight, holding on to faith and a good conscience. Some have rejected these and so have shipwrecked their faith.

—1 TIMOTHY 1:18-19

A PASTOR'S HEART

Reading and reflecting on the story of Sabir and Kalila's family was probably difficult for you. The response from my "focus group" (my wife) was to put down the book and not finish the story. I get it. I understand the difficulty. It's painful to read. The story was equally disturbing to write because it is actual reality and is occurring to our Christian brothers and sisters around the world.

I fought against the good advice of the focus group to soften the story or to leave it out because it forces us to consider the great cost we might have to pay to remain faithful to God in a spiritual disaster. More than helping us understand our possible losses, knowing that there are actual "Sabirs" both in history and today tells us that remaining faithful is worth the unfathomable cost. Faithfulness is worth our lives. It's even worth the toll it could take upon those we love and who are under our care.

So on one hand that story was heartbreaking to write, but on another it was necessary because, as a teacher of Scripture, I know that the principle it demonstrates is true. Scripture makes clear that faithfulness to God outweighs all the costs, but as with all teachings in Christianity, there must be a wielding of both truth and love. Neither is meant to be compromised. As a Bible teacher, I must focus on the unyielding truth; however, as a pastor, I need to also operate out of an unwavering love—both in equal measure.

This causes me to wonder what instruction a pastor might give in real situations such as Sabir's. Remember my account of the Iraqi pastor who told his people not to deny Jesus even when he knew they'd be killed? He didn't encourage them to make such a decision because he wanted them to die, but rather because he loved them. Pastors spend much of their ministries praying for and helping hurting church members. They do this not only because they love their flocks but because their greatest concern is that people are right with God. A truly loving pastor is more concerned about his congregation's souls than about their physical lives.

Of course, a pastor should first be concerned with the destination of his congregants' souls—that they have trusted

Christ as their Savior and will spend eternity in heaven. But that pastor should also be concerned about the day-to-day condition of their souls—that they are living such that when they see Jesus face-to-face, they will hear, "Well done, good and faithful servant." (See Matt. 25:14–30.)

Pastors in the Middle East tell their congregations not to deny Christ.

American pastors need to urge their congregations to continue to stand by their convictions even when legal action is threatened against them, and to be true to Scripture in spite of the political pressure all around them.

Since being right with God is the only hope for humanity and a future in heaven, *this* pastor is consumed with the message found in Matthew 24:10 and other "forgotten prophecies," and that is why I am writing to warn you: our spiritual doomsday is coming.

## MY HEART

For the past four years, as I've prayed over my preaching schedule, I have found that I keep returning to the same topic. To me this topic is an explanation for the greatest heartbreak I've faced in ministry. The subject is also what I've come to believe is the most imminent danger in the American church. It's what keeps me up at night, and the reason I've missed so much time with my wife, my daughters, and my favorite fishing hole to write this book.

The greatest hurt I've faced in ministry wasn't a onetime event but is an ongoing recurrence. The pain began when I was youth council president in tenth grade and continues now as I teach seminary classes. For example, in that earlier time a younger student in my home church's student ministry told me he wanted to give everything to God and live a sold-out life for Him, but then, a few months later he had decided he would never step into youth group or church again. He'd gone from seeking to be a shining witness at school to becoming a notorious partier. Recently, I spent a semester with a young ministry student who was also determined to serve God wholeheartedly. Yet, weeks after the class, he disappeared into the world, wrapped up in his job. He and his family dropped out of church. So far he's not pursued ministry.

Throughout my ministry I've worked with well-meaning, sincere individuals who'd come to the Lord and desired to follow Him wholeheartedly. They were growing in their faith. God was moving in a mighty way and blessing them. They'd be so close to bursting through the challenges they faced and were about to make a tremendous impact for the kingdom; then—poof—they were gone. A few have returned to God, but most haven't. It's painful because I know without a doubt that the words of Matthew 13:44 are true: the kingdom of heaven, won only through a relationship with Jesus, is the greatest treasure in the world. It is worth everything. My heart shatters watching people I love walk away from the great treasure.

I guess I can take comfort in knowing that the statistics show this phenomenon isn't a result of my failed ministry alone. Statistics show that millennials are leaving the church "in droves,"[1] This revelation along with the study revealed in the previous chapter of millions not practicing their faith is surely an epidemic, but it's not an unexplainable one. It is simply the fulfillment of Matthew 24:10 and other scriptures. The missing millions are part of the "many" prophesied in this verse.

These passages haunt me. In my haunted dreams I'm standing before a congregation I dearly love, and a large group of them disappear after facing challenges to their faith. Though it crushes me, I realize that, but for the grace of God, I easily could be one of those many. It's possible you could too.

In the past, preachers spoke of a coming Great Apostasy, when many would turn from the faith. They described it as an event that would be completely evident at the end of the age. How can the millions who have now disappeared from their faith *not* be connected to that prophesied Great Apostasy? The Barna Group recently reported that self-described Christians account for *three out of five* of the adults in America who don't attend church, and somewhere between four thousand and seven thousand churches close their doors every year.[2] The minimum number of nonpracticing Christians in the United States mentioned earlier as 42 million equals more than the total number of Christians in the United Kingdom.[3] In 2010 only thirteen other countries in the world have over 42 million Christians.[4]

From the understanding of the Great Apostasy in the past, we've been looking for a vivid wave of dissent, but the epidemic of apostasy appears to be a silent killer. A faith apocalypse is occurring, and for the most part we remain oblivious to it, trying to solve it through church growth strategies and entertainment rather than understanding these statistics from Scripture. If this "turning away" were a life-threatening disease, such as Ebola, we'd be warned, and there would be measures taken to protect us and help us survive.

My goal, by sharing these scriptural warnings, is that we can prepare to survive the disaster with our faith intact.

Please understand: I don't believe "church" is the epitome

of our faith. We're instructed in Hebrews 10:25 to continue meeting together, but church attendance isn't the most crucial aspect of our following of Christ. I view church as a visual manifestation of our faith. Think of an iceberg. About 90 percent of an iceberg is hidden under the water. The same is true with our faith. Most of it is internal and not visible. But if an iceberg exists, there will be a portion, albeit small, that will be visual. The same is true with our relationship with Christ. If it exists, there should be a portion that's visible. Our participation in church is part of that above-water section. In creating criteria for "practicing" and "nonpracticing" Christians, the Barna Group recognized church attendance as a key factor.[5]

It is important to understand that even in the height of our walk with God, we will face spiritual disasters and could turn away. In fact, no matter how strong we are in our Christian walk, spiritual disasters will come, and the practice of our faith then might be in jeopardy. It's simple cause and effect.

A dear friend of mine whom I'll call Carl was once a strong leader in his church, a supporter of my ministry, and a great witness for Christ in his city. Now he's one of millions who are no longer in church. He still professes to be a Christian, and I know he's truly saved. In fact, I'm 100 percent certain of his salvation. Presently, though, he's not practicing his faith in any way other than occasionally praying before a meal, which also is fading. He believes he's fine, and that one day he'll get back in church. The months have now turned into years.

Though I agree that his eternal security is sure, there is a ripple effect of him not practicing his faith—an effect that fifteen years ago he'd have despised. And when he sees Jesus face-to-face, he'll greatly regret this hopefully short-term lapse.

I want to share a letter with you that I wish I'd written to him fifteen years back.

## A LOVE LETTER

Dear friend and partner in ministry,

More than anything I want you to know I love you, and want only the best for you in life. It's because I care so much about you that I'm writing you this letter. I can't thank you enough for your friendship and the support. I thank you for the times you seek me out to encourage me and support my family in ministry. I'm being blessed through you.

I'm so thankful for your commitment to God. You live out an amazing example for me and others to follow. There are many young men like me who are walking with the Lord today because of your godly example. Your fire for God is evident. Your life clearly expresses that you have a heart for Him. I know you truly know Him and walk with Him.

I'm certain you pray, because God has often revealed His will to you. I remember when you approached me once to offer to make a purchase for our ministry and it was exactly what we needed and had been praying about. God has answered your prayers several times when I asked you to pray with me on certain things. The Lord has often given you just the right words to share with me and other leaders within our ministry.

You read your Bible. I can't count the number of times you've shared with me what the Lord revealed to you in your Bible reading. Often, I have called you in the middle of your Bible study.

Your attitude reveals God is working in your life. Your actions reveal you've been walking with God. I have been amazed at some of the hard decisions you've made as a result of prompting from the Spirit. In addition, you serve the Lord in so many ways. I might need to be writing to you to slow down. I'm not sure there is anything within the church you aren't doing. You're teaching. Working with children and teenagers. Driving the bus. Helping with property upkeep, and you continue to serve as an elder for the church.

Your giving is evidence of your faith in the Lord. You've single-handedly kept a parachurch organization afloat. Faithfully and sacrificially you give to kingdom work.

I have heard your testimony on several occasions, and I have no doubts about your salvation. You're constantly revealing fruit from it. I know you have an unwavering faith in God and a desire to be sold out to Him. I see it. Never can I imagine that changing with you. You've served the Lord faithfully for years.

With my confidence in your faith and walk with God, this letter may seem pointless, but even with your strong faith, there are prophecies in the Bible that cause me to consider that both you and I could falter in our walks with God. These prophecies warn us that difficulties and changes in life will challenge our faith. I know you know them. You taught a series of lessons on some of these.

Although I know we have talked about them, and even taught them, I haven't realized they were prophecies of the same proportions as those that tell of Jesus returning, the Antichrist rising, and amazing signs occurring. We have talked about the end times often. We attended a prophecy conference and spent the drive home talking about what we heard. Because they're in Scripture, we trust they'll occur. We talked about how we need to prepare.

Just as prophecies talk about the physical doomsday, there are passages that warn of a spiritual doomsday. Now, I believe your faith is strong enough to stand firm when faced with these challenges. I believe I'll be strong enough too, but after reading more about these warnings, I believe they apply to us, too. I believe even with our commitment to God, we could fail to be faithful. I find myself wondering what is wrong with people who fail to stand strong. I find myself echoing Peter's words in Matthew 26. Jesus told the disciples they'd turn away when He was arrested and crucified. Peter boldly said, "Even if all fall away . . . I never will." He went on to say, "Even if I have to die . . . I will never disown you" (vv. 33, 35). This was just a few hours before his three denials.

Like us, Peter thought falling away was impossible. He loved Jesus and believed He was the Son of God. He had the best of intentions. He thought others might turn away, but not him. Then Jesus was arrested, imprisoned, and tried. Peter followed Jesus and stood nearby at a fire with his life on the line. Peter stumbled. He turned away. He was unfaithful by denying belonging to Jesus. If Peter wasn't strong enough, how can we think we can be strong enough?

Peter did this while he was possibly in sight of Jesus. Peter was a best friend with Jesus. He was Jesus' "go-to" man. He traveled and lived with Jesus for three years. Peter had witnessed wonder after wonder performed by Jesus. He saw Him heal, feed five thousand, command the waves and wind to cease their roaring, walk on water, teach with authority, give sight to the blind, and raise Lazarus from the dead. He had conversation after conversation with Jesus. He laughed with him. Peter knew Jesus like no one else—but he still turned away.

If even Peter did this, then it's possible for us to. Peter's falling away was only momentary, no more than forty days, but I don't even want to do that, or for that to happen to you.

Although I hope to be faithful, I know there have been so many times I have given in to temptation or wasn't obedient to the prompting of the Spirit. These were failures and momentary lapses of my faith. That's why I want to warn you.

Here are the spiritual disasters that those critical prophecies warn about:

- a weakened church
- an unchallenged faith
- a sinful culture
- spiritual warfare
- the temptation of possessions and position
- persecution
- spiritual entropy
- spiritual amnesia
- difficult trials in life
- sexual temptations
- false teachings
- hurt feelings
- complacency
- disillusionment

I love you and know that this isn't what you want for your life. I know the best thing in your life is your relationship with God, and I know you agree. So please don't let go of that. Please hear these warnings.

Even if you stumble, as the prophecies suggest, that doesn't mean your salvation is lost, but I know you want to hear Jesus say, he is pleased of your faithful endurance for eternity, your faithfulness to God and denial of your flesh will matter greatly to you.

Your faithfulness is very important not only in eternity, but now. I need you to be spiritually strong to help me and my family. Your wife needs a husband who walks with God and leads the home spiritually. Your children need your strong spiritual leadership. Your grandchildren need a godly grandparent. They need the spiritual legacy you have been passing down to your children, and that's been passed down to you. Your church needs you to remain faithful. I know you grow weary of all you do, but it isn't in vain. You'd be surprised how much strength you give your church.

Your city also needs you. They don't know they're lost. They need you to keep a faithful personal witness. Your coworkers in the office need Christ. They've been watching you. Your best friend, who you've prayed would come to Christ for years, is going to finally come to church and come to the Lord. He needs you to disciple him. You have no idea how much your faithfulness will affect the generations to follow. You have no idea the domino effect that impacts others around your life.

Although these prophecies are written to me and you, we can overcome.

Please hear my warning because it will happen subtly. If you're not careful, when trials come, you'll slowly stop practicing your faith, and your heart will harden. Please prepare. Just as you have a storm shelter for a tornado, prepare a shelter for your faith. Just as you always carry tools, jumper cables, spare tires, and jacks in your vehicle—prepare for these spiritual disasters. Please promise me you will prepare.

Out of a love for you and a passion for Jesus,

Jake

### SAVED LIVES

Not only do I wish I could've warned Carl with this letter, but I hope to warn you. We're not immune. I wish I'd written this letter more than a decade ago when he was at the height of his spiritual life, possibly where you are now. He was at a place in his life in which he never thought he'd turn away from the practice of his faith, but he did.

Scripture doesn't only tell us we'll face these spiritual disasters; it also tells us how we'll fare. It's not a pretty picture. The aftermath of a spiritual doomsday is a horrific scene, much like the scene of the path of an F5 tornado, the epicenter of a large earthquake, or ground zero of a bomb blast.

A large, F4 tornado recently hit a city nearby. The devastation was unimaginable. Homes, businesses, shopping centers, and entire subdivisions in its path were obliterated. Eighteen people were killed, which is absolutely tragic, but with the strength of that tornado, the death toll could've been much higher. One family lost their brick home, and even after three weeks they still hadn't found their refrigerator. Their washer and dryer were found in small pieces. Surveyors of the wreckage contribute lives saved to preparatory measures the community had taken in the three-year period before the storm.

The same city had been hit three years earlier—almost to the day. In those three years, the town heeded the warnings of the event reoccurring and *prepped*. Many of the homes that were rebuilt or newly built during those three years were required to have a safe room or a storm shelter. Large community safe rooms were built in local schools. During the storm one of these shelters housed three hundred people. Those were three hundred lives saved because the community had *prepped*. The local area and entire state had worked to create quicker and more effective warnings. All of this saved lives.

Denying the possibilities of another tornado would have been easy for this particular community. After all, what were the odds of a tornado hitting the exact area twice?

Brother or sister in Christ, Scripture tells us we will be hit with spiritual storm after spiritual storm.

Are we heeding the warnings?

## DON'T FORGET GRACE

This book is meant to be a warning. It is meant to save you the frustration and lost time of faithfulness, but please don't let the strong warning veil the grace God offers to us. My friend can come back to church and a passionate walk with Christ at any time. God will meet him on the road miles ahead of the house. The Lord will place upon him the robe and ring of salvation and the joy that follows. The fattened calf will be slaughtered and celebration will ring out in heaven, just as it was in Jesus' parable of the prodigal son. (See Luke 15:11–32.)

God is like that. He is abounding in love, grace, and mercy. He forgives. He restores.

If you find yourself like my friend and the many others whose stories are told in this book, return to faithfulness. God will meet you and restore you. You are never too far gone. I know there is a chance God's miraculous grace could be missed in this book, but what I feel I must argue is that those who are not practicing their faith are prodigal sons and daughters. They may still refer to themselves as sons or daughters and still have a fondness for the Father, but when they see Him in the age to come, they will wish they had not lived unfaithfully.

In the same spirit, if you have a loved one who has turned away from the faith, don't give up on him or her. Be the loving father in the prodigal son parable. Look for and pray for that friend or family member to return to faithfulness, and know that it is possible. God does not give up on His people. He answers prayer, and for that reason I want to pray for you.

A PRAYER

Dear Father,

I am grateful to have the opportunity to write this book, and I am amazed that someone would pick it up, and even more so, read it. I pray for the one holding this book, that he or she would see You as the great treasure, worthy of everything. If the reader has accepted your gift of salvation, I pray that you would remind him or her of how valuable that gift is. Please remind this precious soul of how much he or she will want to hear "Well done, My good and faithful servant" upon seeing You. If the reader has not accepted your gift, I pray that you would convict this son or daughter and draw him or her to You, to a relationship with You.

Regardless of how much of a spiritual high this reader may sit upon, would You let this warning penetrate his or her heart, bringing the realization that he or she could be one of the many who turn away? Will You bring a dread of this disaster and lead this son or daughter to prep spiritually?

If he or she has already turned from faithfulness, will You call this son or daughter back home and back to faithfulness? Please assure him or her of your embrace and the celebration that follows.

You are worth our sweat, blood, and perseverance—remind us, oh, Lord.

In the name of Jesus, amen.

# SPIRITUAL PREPPER'S CHECKLIST

As you prepare to be faithful, keep these three things in mind.

☐ Realize YOU could turn away.

This point has been presented throughout this chapter, but still we all struggle to realize just how quickly we can turn away. While we have incredible strength through Christ, we are still weak in our sinful nature. That is why Paul admonishes the Corinthians to "Be on your guard; stand firm in the faith; be courageous; be strong" (1 Corinthians 16:13).

Church leaders this reality needs to shape your ministry models. We need to consciously protect our people.

☐ Build accountability into your life.

Any one of us could be one who turns away. We need to protect ourselves. We have to let others into our lives that can hold us accountable. We have to put ourselves in "systems" of accountability. The starting point is a church. Get plugged into a Bible-believing-and-teaching church. Don't just attend Sunday services, but rather take the next step and join a small group, life group, Bible study, or Sunday school class. It's in the smaller settings where you meet people who can walk through life with us. Consider volunteering in your local church so that those ministry leaders are holding us accountable.

☐ Learn to give yourself an honest self-assessment.

James gives a picture of what the deception looks like by telling of a man who sees himself clearly in the mirror, but walks away forgetting what he just saw. (See James 1:23–24.) It is hard to reflect honestly upon our own lives, but we need to develop that skill. Take time to examine your life. When you see an area in which you are trying to control yourself, to do your own will, or seek your own pleasure, make the necessary changes to submit to the Lord: confess, repent, and submit. To develop the skill assess yourself and compare it to those who hold you accountable.

As a follower of Christ such self-reflection is not only up to us. We have the Holy Spirit who is our Guide and Convictor. When we walk in step with the Holy Spirit, He shows us what we need to do, but we have to make the necessary responses.

# 3

# PREPPING FOR PERSECUTION

In the last days scoffers will come, scoffing and following their own evil desires. They will say, "Where is this 'coming' he promised?"

2 PETER 3:3–4

## A FORECASTED SPIRITUAL DISASTER

This morning I hit my knees early to pray for a dear friend, a member of the church I pastor, who was having a high-risk surgery. My soul was heavy for the surgery, her health, and for her husband and children, who would be by her side. I longed for God to heal and protect her. I prayed for those things, but I had a concern even greater than her physical survival.

My concern was her *faith*.

My prayer was for the perseverance of her husband's faith.

It was her young children's future walk with Christ and the

faith of her many friends who would wait by the phone that tugged at my heart. So I prayed not only for a successful surgery and complete recovery, but more than anything for the faith of my friend, her family, her friends, and those on the sidelines. I prayed their faith would not falter, but rather, would grow and strengthen, because our relationship with Jesus matters most. Preparation for eternity is of greater concern than how well we physically survive this life.

The night before, I visited with a friend who was going through a divorce. I felt for him and his family. There were so many considerations, but I skipped everything and boldly told him, "Please, no matter what, don't let this diminish your faith."

I hate both of those situations and the many others I encounter as a pastor, but unfortunately they're part of this life. Jesus said in Matthew 6:34, "Each day has . . . trouble."

Difficult trials are life for us all, but it's especially the case for the Christian. The apostle Peter wrote that followers of Jesus shouldn't be shocked by attacks on their faith. First Peter 4:12–13 says, "Dear friends, do not be surprised at the painful trial you are suffering, as though something strange were happening to you. But rejoice that you participate in the sufferings of Christ, so that you may be overjoyed when his glory is revealed." We must keep Peter's words in front of us because these trials can derail our faithful following of Christ. One of these spiritual disasters that Peter forecasted is persecution, just as Jesus prophesied earlier in Matthew 24:9–10.

By the time of Jesus' prophecy, His disciples had already seen a glimpse of the world's hatred of Jesus, and were soon to taste the full outright bitterness when Jesus was arrested, falsely accused, unfairly tried, and crucified. Seeing this persecution firsthand, realizing they were probably next, became a pivotal moment for the disciples—a moment in which they temporarily failed in their faith and hid. The fear of the unknown and the possible loss of their lives created a spiritual disaster for them and momentarily eclipsed the practice of their faith.

Jesus didn't hide in fine print the fact that following Him might cost us our lives. He was very clear about it. We find Him teaching on it in the Gospels. Then in Acts and the Epistles we read of the effects of persecution. The story of the first Christians is a story of persecution, first from their own people, the Jews, and then from the Romans. (At times there would even be persecution from *inside* the church.) The New Testament closes with those first-century Christians in the middle of some of the most intense persecution in history. The very purpose of the book of Revelation was to encourage the early church to keep their faith in the midst of fierce slaughter on account of their faith.

Almost every biblical warning of persecution is paired with strong encouragements to endure and overcome. This encouragement proves that in the midst of persecution there is a temptation and a high possibility of abandoning our faith. Although we have accounts of bold Christians who held on to their faith even in martyrdom, there must be many more accounts of those who were scared off at the first sign of harassment.

But we have been warned. Those around us will not always take kindly to our faith. The apostle Peter wrote:

> First of all, you must understand that in the last days scoffers will come, scoffing and following their own evil desires. They will say, "Where is this 'coming' he promised? Ever since our

fathers died, everything goes on as it has since the beginning of creation." But they deliberately forget that long ago by God's word the heavens existed and the earth was formed out of water and by water. By these waters also the world of that time was deluged and destroyed. By the same word the present heavens and earth are reserved for fire, being kept for the Day of Judgment and destruction of ungodly men. (2 Peter 3:3–9)

A "scoffer" is one who mocks the belief of another, and Peter has warned us that "scoffers" in the last days will venomously attack Scripture, the teachings of Christ, and Christians themselves.

Who said words don't hurt? The words of a scoffer will hurt for eternity for some. Persecution isn't only delivered by a sword, a gun, a lion, or a stake. It can come in the form of ridicule so cruel that it turns even the strongest away from their faith—it leads them to spiritual disaster.

## JEFF'S SPIRITUAL DISASTER

Jeff was one of the godliest persons I've ever been around. He had a deep passion for Jesus, for people, and for evangelism. He also had this uncanny knack for building sincere relationships and sharing Christ through them.

He didn't know me from Adam when he befriended me. He was a campus ministry director at a university, but I didn't even go to his school. Yet he still befriended me and continually encouraged me in ministry for years.

His college ministry was neither splashy nor was it the largest on campus, but it was definitely the deepest. He was used of God to produce some the most theologically rooted college students in the nation. There were very few who graduated from his ministry who didn't end up church planting or on a foreign mission field. Jeff and his wife always had students at their house, seeking out answers about God's direction for their lives.

After several years of leading that campus ministry, Jeff felt called to attend seminary. During his time at seminary, he believed God had revealed that he needed to work toward being a professor at a secular university. He felt called to stand for truth in a hostile environment, and believed God could use him to organically reach students with the gospel.

Jeff excelled at seminary and graduated with high honors. He was then accepted by a highly distinguished university for doctoral work. He was outstanding in his field of study, considered an expert even while still in school.

One of the last times I saw Jeff, he told me how God had opened the door for him to carry out research in a field of study that intersected with Scripture. He was excited about the good that could come through his work, believing he could vindicate Scripture and help others have a greater understanding.

That wasn't my most recent conversation with Jeff. I checked in with him some time later to tell him, as I'd done many times before, what God was doing in my life. I told him that my wife and I were reading through an awesome devotional on prayer and about how we'd been praying together for particular guidance in our life. I was shocked by his response. Unashamedly he said, "Jake, God doesn't care about our little insignificant lives. You just have to do the wise thing or what you can live with the most."

My response was, "Come back. What?"

He apologized for confronting me, but said that he was fed up with small-minded Christianity. He went on to remind me that he had spent more time with the original language of Scripture than most people spend with the English text in an entire lifetime. He then said that after visiting over coffee or lunch with some of the world's most renowned scholars, he had decided that he'd been wrong back when he was a campus minister. "Yes, I still think there had to be an intelligent creator of this world, but it's foolish to believe God is involved in our everyday details."

I was shocked.

After I hung up the phone, I sat frozen in disbelief long enough for my wife to notice. Of course she had to know details, but I didn't have enough, so she called another mutual friend of Jeff and his wife, Elizabeth, and got the full scoop. Elizabeth had shared with our friend that she was coming around to Jeff's way of thinking. They had quit attending the church plant they had helped establish. They did still go to church, but it was a church that brought in speakers from the university to give insightful "lectures."

Jeff's views had shifted while he was writing papers to submit to a biblical studies scholar organization. The papers had to be strictly scholarly. From that work and from conversations with his newfound, secular influences, he changed his entire belief system. He also stopped the practice of his faith. He no longer sought to reach others and to help provide insight into Scripture. Now he sought to be the world's most renowned scholar in his field. The most telling statement came from Elizabeth. She told my wife, "No one takes you serious as a scholar if you believe in the inspiration of Scripture, miracles, the virgin birth, or even Jesus being more than a historic teacher. You can't profess to be a Christian and be respected in the circles Jeff is being accepted in."

Scoffers had caused Jeff to turn from his faith. This was Jeff's spiritual disaster.

## THE AFTERMATH

What happened in Jeff's life is common. Scoffing is becoming more prevalent as the eschatological clock ticks closer to the return of Jesus. Many have fallen as Jeff has fallen—some through scholarship, but also from other circumstances of life. I'm praying this isn't a permanent position for Jeff and Elizabeth. God can pull them out of this breach of faithfulness. He'll forgive them and use them again for His glory, but right now it appears that Jeff has met with a spiritual doomsday. Worse, though he assumes it's only affecting him, that's far from the truth.

None of our lives are isolated. We're all interconnected, like dominos lined up in a row. When we move in our faith, whether forward or backward, those around us and even those far away are affected.

The fallout from Jeff's departure from his faith began in his home. He has pulled Elizabeth away from her faithful relationship with Jesus. I also know Jeff's extended family are all nonbelievers. He had worked on them for years. He told me once that his dad was finally coming around, but Jeff's new direction has halted his dad—and the rest of his family—from coming to Christ for now, and possibly forever. The couple don't have children yet, but they hope to. If they do, now their children will grow up in a home where Christianity won't be practiced, and they may never hear the gospel from their parents.

As a friend, I'm discouraged in my own faith through Jeff's turning aside. I can't imagine how this has affected his former students. Will some of them turn from their faith through the influence of their mentor? The church plant that Jeff helped start is reeling in confusion over his change.

I also think of those who won't hear the gospel or see the example of a faithful Jeff. He was a champion evangelist. What about those future students he'll now lead astray through his current teachings? I hope Jeff comes back to fully practicing his faith, but in the meantime damage is being done.

## PERSECUTION BY EXCLUSION

Scoffing doesn't only occur in the academic ivory towers. It can also occur at the local Sonic, as it did for Simone.

We had gathered in a room off the side of the stage. The evangelist had instructed us "encouragers" to lead those who came forward during the altar call into this room to speak to them further. Simone had come forward.

Simone came to Sunday school almost weekly, though I'm sure it was because her parents made her do so. She occasionally attended the student ministry worship service, but sat in the back with her cheerleader friends and glared. They definitely felt they were too cool to be there. But here she was, having responded to an altar call.

Simone told me she'd trusted Christ as her Savior. "Pastor Jake, I was saved when I was nine, she said. "I know that it was real." But with tears rolling down her checks, she went on to say, "But I haven't been living the way I should. I'm lukewarm, like the speaker talked about today. I want to give God everything, and I'm rededicating my life to him."

She was serious. She didn't waste any time following through with her rededication either. Here was the captain of the cheer squad and the most popular girl in school, and she was on fire for God. Immediately, she called her friends and told them about the decision she'd made. Throughout the remainder of the school year, she cleaned up the cheer squad and was working on the football team. Twenty-three, yes twenty-three, of her friends began coming to her youth group. Ten of them trusted Christ as their Savior.

Parties turned into worship services in that small town. The sky was the limit on the impact Simone could have on her school, because she was only a sophomore.

I haven't talked to Simone in the fifteen years that have passed. I've stopped asking former students in that ministry about her and haven't scanned her Facebook profile in some time because it breaks my heart. I know the story though. Hers is a story I know too well, for it played out over and over again while I was a student pastor.

Simone became a passionate, outspoken leader within the student ministry. That summer she spent a week in the Dominican Republic and came back from that mission trip on fire for God. She was passionately in love with Jesus, and was even thinking God might be calling her into missions.

Following the trip, she volunteered for a week at a local church camp, where she poured herself into a group of fourth grade girls. They looked up to her and wanted to be just like her. She fell especially in love with Bethany, a girl who had a rough home life. Then Simone volunteered at her church's vacation Bible school. During that week, she turned sixteen and got a new car. Her first trip alone was to the mall, where she bought Bethany a whole new wardrobe and a cool kids Bible. On Friday afternoon she brought the gifts to Bethany. The little girl lit up like the sun. Simone had never felt better, and she knew living sold out to Christ was what life was about.

After leaving Bethany's home, she pulled into the local teen hangout. Parked in the back were three vehicles and some older high school students. Her friend Abigail was there with her new boyfriend, a senior. Abigail was one of those Simone had brought to youth group. She flagged Simone down; everyone wanted to see her new car. They stood around and talked for almost an hour. As the crew split ways, one of the guys asked Simone to join them at a party that night.

Immediately someone spoke up and said Simone was "too Christian" to go and that she didn't know how to have fun. Simone bowed out of the party, but that night she thought on what had been said.

The next Wednesday she didn't show for youth group. The following Friday afternoon, at that same hangout, history repeated itself. The same guy was there. He said, "I'd ask you to go to party at the lake tonight, but I know Jesus won't *let* you go."

She replied, "I can do whatever the hell I want to do." He smiled and she left her car and hopped in with him. She went to the party that night, then another party on Saturday night, and was too hung over for church Sunday. Her cross necklace came off her neck. Youth group became a thing of the past. She lived to prove she wasn't "too Christian" to have a good time. Her friends never questioned her; they just followed suit. If Simone did something, then it was cool. Scoffing and exclusion had led to Simone's spiritual disaster, perhaps even her spiritual doomsday.

THE AFTERMATH

I had sat in the chair in front of Simone that night after the altar call, and I'm convinced her prayer was real. God had gotten ahold of her, and for a time she was used in a mighty way. But then along came the ridicule, the exclusion, the discrimination, the mild persecution, and her faith was left in the dust. Following that revival service and Simone's rededication to Christ, Simone's life was on a path of joy and blessing. She felt it. We could see the light in her, but now that light is out and is replaced by hurt and guilt. This change in her life wasn't the only repercussion of her turning away.

Now she carries the shame from the life she lived during her remaining years of high school and in college. Not only did she fail to continue reaching her friends with the gospel, but she actually led many away from it. Twenty of the twenty-three who had come to youth group with her eventually left the group. The cheerleading squad, which she had completely transformed, actually turned the opposite direction.

Simone is an adult now, with a career, a husband, and a child. Sadly, all of those major foundational decisions were made outside of a relationship with Christ. She is completely out of church, and her husband isn't a Christian. Her child has never even been in a church, and it appears he won't grow up in a Christian home.

Simone's departure from her faith affected far more than just her, or even her and her family. The spouses and children of those she led astray in high school and college also may not come to know Christ. So her choices didn't affect only one generation, but rather, generations to come. Many of the girls in the classes behind Simone followed her footsteps. The church's student ministry declined, when once Simone had held the influence to help it greatly succeed.

I'm convinced Simone is secure eternally, but in eternity she'll see the effects of her spiritual disaster, set off by the mildest of persecution. Many of her friends and others in her sphere of influence won't be gathered with her around the throne of God.

### THEY WILL EVEN "HATE" YOU

Though no one appeared to hate Simone for following Christ, the Bible is clear that our faithfulness to Jesus will bring not only scorn but outright hatred from those who do not follow Him. He told His first disciples and us:

> If the world hates you, keep in mind that it hated me first. If you belonged to the world, it would love you as its own. As it is, you do not belong to the world, but I have chosen you out of the world. That is why the world hates you. Remember the words I spoke to you: "No servant is greater than his master." If they persecuted me, they will persecute you also. If they obeyed my teaching, they will obey yours also. They will treat you this way because of my name, for they do not know the One who sent me. (John 15:18–21)

This world will hate you and me.

The book of Revelation also warns of this hatred for Christ-followers. Descriptions of Christian persecution flood its pages. For one, the book was written to Christians who were already being heavily persecuted. In fact, they were facing some of the most traumatic persecution ever under the Roman Empire. Christians were being rounded up, imprisoned, beaten, fed to lions, massacred by the gladiators, impaled on stakes, and suffering many other atrocities.

Chapters 2 and 3 of Revelation give us the most practical

teaching on persecution. Those two chapters contain seven letters written to seven real churches, directly from Jesus via the pen of John the apostle. These real churches were facing real problems. Some form of persecution is found in almost every letter, and that persecution threatened to lead them into unfaithfulness. Each church was at a pivotal moment, and their outcome would hinge on how they resolved the conflict they faced. Some of the churches had been faithful in the past and were remaining faithful in the present; others were struggling under the persecution and were at risk of losing their "lampstand," or their faithful witnessam—which I fear for us. Our faithful witness and the amazing blessings that come through a walk with Christ can be lost if the warnings aren't heeded in our own lives.

The church of Ephesus (Rev. 2:1–7) was complimented for their perseverance under pressure. They had "endured hardships" for Christ's name (v. 3). We know from Acts 19 that they faced particular persecution because of their effect on the city's economy.

The church at Thyatira (Rev. 2:18–29) was faltering because of their embrace of false teaching. The city of Thyatira was strongly influenced by trade guilds. Anyone who wanted a job, a career, or an income needed to belong to a guild. Each guild had a patron god that they worshipped. The worship involved idolatry and sexual immorality. Christians faced intense pressure to participate. When they refused, they lost their jobs and their income, and were unable to make a living. So they were tempted to accept false teaching to alleviate the persecution they faced.

The letter to the church at Philadelphia (Rev. 3:7–13) offers a compliment to them for enduring. No doubt, persecution was a part of what they endured, because they were praised for not having denied Christ's name, something they were likely pressured to do.

The church of Pergamum (Rev. 2:12–17) suffered the loss of a church member and probable leader, Antipas. Yet, even when their fellow saint was martyred, most of them remained faithful.

The letter to the church of Smyrna (Rev. 2:8–11) reveals that persecution had made life harder for them and had led to poverty. Yet, they remained faithful, even when slandered. They were excluded from families, wills, synagogues, jobs, and even from conducting business due to their faith in Christ. As if this weren't enough, they were told they'd face even greater persecution. Their lives would be at stake. They'd be killed for their faith. But Jesus told them to "be faithful, even to the point of death" (v. 10).

If you're in America, you've been able to begin following Christ and remain faithful to Him without much suffering. Your life hasn't been threatened each day, so thoughts of martyrdom may have never crossed your mind. This makes it difficult to understand passages like these. But persecution has begun in the United States. Yours will not be by the sword, or with a mass grave awaiting you, but like Jeff, you may find that you are not taken seriously because of your faith. Like Simone, you may be made fun of, or excluded from the inner circle. Remember: persecution isn't just imprisonment or death. As seen in Revelation, it also manifests through discrimination (not being hired, being passed up for a promotion, or even losing a job), slander, scoffing, and the list goes on. The point is, persecution is here, and it's intensifying. We must simply remain faithful when we are faced with it.

Persecution may spell a spiritual doomsday for many, but it doesn't have to for you or for me. We can overcome. We can remain faithful. We just have to prepare ourselves.

# SPIRITUAL PREPPER'S CHECKLIST

Throughout the book, you will see how the items on the check-lists could have changed the game for the individuals in the examples. If Christians were more aware of the temptation to deny the supernatural, especially in the academic arena, maybe they would be stronger as they face challenges. In many youth groups there are often lessons on how peer pressure can affect a Christian, but the seriousness of the cost of turning is not always made clear.

☐ Be tough.

Olympians sacrifice most of their childhood and much of their life to train so that they may compete. The same is true for great athletes, musicians, scientists, or people in any field. They commit and make sacrifices. They stay focused and work hard. We need to apply this to our Christian walk. We need to be tough. We need to stick to what we believe even in the face of mocking and verbal abuse. Read stories of the heroes of the faith who persevered through great diffi-culty, such as Martin Luther, John Wesley, Amy Carmichael, Corrie Ten Boom, or Jim Elliott.

☐ Prioritize your fears.

Jeff and Simone were afraid of being left out by their peers, which is all too familiar for us in our Christian walk. The fear of what others will think of us often holds us back. Our actions should be motivated by fear, but not fear of man. We should love and respect God, but we should also fear God and eternal judgment.

☐ Study Christian martyrdom.

Some churches hold discipleship classes or Sunday school classes. They usually cover particular books of the Bible or topics like evangelism, discipleship, missions, or Christian history. It is important, however, that we keep the topic of persecution and martyrdom before us. Consider book-marking some great websites that chronicle the martyrs today: The Voice of the Martyrs (persecution.com), Open Doors USA (opendoorsusa.org), International Christian Concern (Persecution.org), Barnabas Aid (barnabasfund.org), and Rescue Christians (rescuechristians.org).

Consider subscribing to newsletters and participating in the International Day of Prayer for the Persecuted Church. Read the books *Foxe's Book of Martyrs*, *I Am N*, and *Tortured for Christ*. Keep the persecuted church in your mind, and it will help you be spiritually prepared for persecution.

# 4

# PREPPING FOR MORE PERSECUTION

"You will be handed over to be persecuted and put to death, and you will be hated by all nations because of me. At that time many will turn away from the faith."

MATTHEW 24:9–10

## A FORECASTED SPIRITUAL DISASTER

The atmosphere was tense.

Urgency was in His voice.

Change was in the air.

Jesus sat down for one more meal with His disciples before He was to leave them for a little while. The disciples had no idea what lay ahead. In a couple of hours, their Master, their friend, the one they believed to be the promised Messiah and whom they'd staked their lives upon, would be arrested. Before their eyes He'd go to trial, and they'd witness complete injustice. They'd see Jesus receive a brutal beating, and the following day they would watch Him hang on a cross upon Golgotha.

These men watched Jesus die and be placed in a tomb. Their friend. Their hope. Their future was gone.

If their leader had been arrested, unfairly tried, brutally beaten, and crucified—then they certainly were next.

They faced an uncertain, pivotal moment.

A spiritual disaster had come upon them, and they'd failed, but the disaster shouldn't have been a surprise to them. It had been forecasted. Granted, the warning had come only a few hours ahead of the faith-shaking disaster.

At that last supper Jesus told the disciples around the table with Him that they'd turn away. "This very night," He said, "you will all fall away on account of me, for it is written: 'I will strike the shepherd, and the sheep of the flock will be scattered'" (Matt. 26:31). He even warned that one of them (Judas) would betray Him (v. 21), and that Peter, specifically, would disown Him, not once, but three times (v. 34).

And Peter did exactly that.

## PETER'S SPIRITUAL DISASTER

When soldiers came to arrest Jesus, Peter initially showed boldness, drawing his sword and even slicing off a soldier's ear. But Jesus had already been given the kiss of betrayal by Judas, and he was taken prisoner.

There must have been an eerie silence when the light of the soldiers' torches faded in the distance. With Jesus gone, Peter and the rest of the disciples were left clueless. There was probably a tense discussion among them. They had to think they were next. Nine or ten of them decided to run and hide. Only two chose to stick near Jesus.

Peter and John trailed Jesus. They gained access into the courtyard of the high priest where Jesus was being tried. It was in that courtyard that the promised challenge came upon Peter. Recognized for who he was, Peter was asked point-blank if he was a disciple. Terrified, he denied it—three times.

The rooster's crow ended the scene (Matt. 26:74), clarifying that Peter had indeed done exactly what Jesus had said he'd do. He'd let the fear of persecution cause him to adamantly deny the one he believed to be the Son of God. We know the outcome of Peter's spiritual disaster. It could have been a spiritual doomsday for him. Thankfully, it wasn't.

## THE AFTERMATH

In theologian and professor D. A. Carson's commentary on the gospel of John, he refers to Peter's denial of Christ as a "lapse."[1] Carson has captured the event perfectly. Peter didn't stop believing in Jesus. His disobedience was momentary, and he stopped practicing his faith only for a time. Within forty days of viewing the empty tomb, Peter had experienced a formal restoration with Jesus. The damage from his failure of faith was minimal, but to the grave and into eternity I'm sure there is nothing Peter would regret more.

Had Peter remained faithful, he could have kept the other disciples encouraged, but due to his faith lapse, they stayed discouraged. Their captain was unable to rally the troops. Who knows what kind of impact Peter could have had if he'd stood boldly during this time. The greatest effect of the denial was that Peter would have to live with it, and can I assume with confidence that Satan used that faith lapse to discourage Peter throughout the rest of his ministry. He had let down his friend and his Lord.

The faithfulness Peter showed following his repentance more than made up for that lapse of faith. Yet, you know that when we meet Peter in eternity, he will tell us that the biggest regret in his life was his folding under the threat of persecution and denying Jesus.

Peter missed an opportunity to experience a "God moment." If he had been bold under pressure, God would have protected him. This would've strengthened the faith of other followers and declared God's glory. But he failed. Even so, Peter did not experience a spiritual doomsday.

Judas's failure of faith *was* his spiritual doomsday. He committed suicide soon after selling Jesus out. It wasn't the suicide that doomed Judas, though, but rather, that he never truly humbled himself to accept Jesus as his Lord and Savior. Jesus made this distinction clear in John 6:70 and in John 17:12.

It is important for us to understand the difference between Peter's failure and Judas's, and what it meant for each of them. Matthew 24:10, which has been our key verse thus far, says that many will turn away due to persecution. It's hard to reconcile this turning away with the security of the believer. The question becomes, if someone "turns away," does he lose his salvation? Or, if someone is able to "turn away," does that mean she wasn't truly saved?

Jesus had both of these situations in his audience at the Last Supper. It was as if Judas wasn't truly saved while the other eleven were all truly born again. But Jesus' warning to them about falling away applied to both his and the other disciples' cases. Judas was being warned that his turning away would result in a complete *end* of his faith. Theoretically, Judas could have repented and the disaster not been his doomsday. The eleven, on the other hand did "turn away," but it was only from the *practice* of their faith.

Some who turn away aren't truly born again, and never were. They fit the profile of Matthew 7:21–23:

> "Not everyone who says to me, 'Lord, Lord,' will enter the kingdom of heaven, but only he who does the will of my Father who is in heaven. Many will say to me on that day, 'Lord, Lord, did we not prophesy in your name, and in your name drive out demons and perform many miracles?' Then I will tell them plainly, 'I never knew you. Away from me, you evildoers!'"

Judas wouldn't have been surprised upon hearing this when arriving at the gate of eternity. He had to know he had never truly humbled himself and bowed his heart to Jesus. As for Peter and the others, there are consequences that follow faith failures. We may remain secure with regard to eternity, but our desire shouldn't be simply to be happy to be in heaven by the "skin of our teeth." The only reason anyone is in heaven is through faith, but I perceive that many of us entertain the sentiment that we'll be happy to just be there. But I promise you, when you see Jesus, you'll desire to hear the that you have kept the faith. Your faithfulness will matter greatly to you at that point.

Our faithfulness will also determine our rewards in heaven, and maybe even our roles in the millennial kingdom. Often scripture indicates that if we're faithful in the small things, then we'll be given more. (See Matt. 25:14–30; Luke 16:10.) This is a clear practical occurrence now, but it may also foreshadow the thousand-year reign of Christ on earth.

But let's get back to Peter for a moment.

The threat of persecution would chase Peter for the rest of his life. He would be opposed, arrested, imprisoned, and beaten for his proclamation of the gospel (see Acts 4:1–22; 5:12–40; 12:1–5). Yet, Peter would never waver again as he did in that courtyard the night of Jesus' arrest. Eventually there would be a final arrest and imprisonment. It would end in martyrdom. Peter still never wavered. This time around he didn't deny Christ. Rather, according to church tradition, he asked to be crucified upside down out of honor and reverence of Jesus.

Peter died as a result of persecution. Only this time, he was prepared against the spiritual disaster that could have come. He stood steadfast in trust of the Lord. At last, remaining faithful and obedient outweighed any fear of persecution that he may have had.

## THE SPOILS OF FAITHFULNESS

Can you imagine how different the start of Christianity would have been if Peter hadn't repented and returned to faithfully follow Christ?

If Peter had let the fear of persecution drive him away from his faith completely, there may not have been three thousand saved in one day on Pentecost just after Jesus' ascension (see Acts 2). He definitely would haven't been the one to preach that day. If he had stopped preaching at the first sign of persecution, the man at the gate called Beautiful would not have been healed nor would any who witnessed that healing have been saved (see 3:2–10). The disciples may not have been as bold as they were. They may have allowed the problems of the early church to engulfed them had Peter not been there and allowed God to use him to provide leadership.

If Peter had completely turned away from God, the gospel would not have come to the Gentiles as early as it did. The good news would have spread, but in the meantime people would have perished without knowing Jesus.

Looking back to the previous chapter, what could God have done through Simone if she had remained faithful? What could God have done through Jeff? What can God still do through both Simone *and* Jeff if they will only repent?

Five of the seven churches of Revelation were at a pivotal moment. Each was on the brink of a spiritual disaster that could drive them away from faithfulness. Several had already started down the path to some degree, but grace was offered: in each case, God's message to them was "Repent." Even a failure in times of persecution doesn't mean you don't have a chance to repent, but the consequences of even short-term unfaithfulness should bother us.

Along with being told to repent the church in Ephesus was instructed that if they continued in their departure from God, He would remove their lampstand. This lampstand represented their faithful witness and the blessings that would come along with being in God's will. Such a result would be devastating to the work of Christ in Ephesus, and in the individual lives of the Ephesian believers. If they would remain faithful they could continue to enjoy those benefits.

Good things—God things—come from our faithfulness.

We receive personal benefits from faithfulness.

We also reap the spoils of the faithfulness of others.

We're recipients of the spoils of Peter's faithfulness even now.

## THE REALITY OF PERSECUTION

As mentioned earlier, Christian persecution definitely didn't end in the first century. It has impacted every generation of Christians since Jesus was arrested in the Garden. Persecution has varied in intensity and location, but it has occurred and is occurring right now.

Ministries that follow contemporary Christian persecution tell us that more persecution is happening today than at any point in history. While you read this, Christians are being killed for their faith. Presently, it's estimated that eleven Christians are killed every hour, and at least one hundred *thousand* Christians are martyred each year. Currently there are 110 countries where Christians are reportedly being persecuted.[2]

Of course, they are not being executed in all 110 nations, but they are being thrown into prison, sentenced to labor camps, or displaced and forced to flee to refugee camps. Yet in these danger zones Christians continue to meet in secret, underground churches, and they continue to remain faithful and share the gospel.

Even with this intense persecution raging around the world, Christians in America haven't encountered it. That appears to be changing, and changing fast. It's for this reason we must be reminded of scriptural prophecies that tell us that persecution will occur and will tempt us to turn away because of it. In the meantime, there's something else we should think about.

In America, we don't have to meet at secret locations. Rather, we have huge buildings and accessible websites—what a contrast. Here we don't have to be afraid to share Christ or to possess a Bible. Yet, what American Christians are facing today is, in many ways, more of a threat to our faith than even what Iraqi Christians are facing at the hands of ISIS. I don't say that to take away from the evil of that brutal slaughter. The persecution of Iraqis and others is more intense and terrifying than anything we have experienced here. Yet, it's the subtle, daily fighting against the grain for the American Christian that proves to be more a threat to one's faith. I say this because there are few stories of Christians who recanted when they faced martyrdom or prison. When a gun is aimed or a sword is drawn, Christians seem to rise to the occasion. In nations where it's illegal for Christians to gather for worship, I'd argue that the believer attends worship more regularly than we do here in the States. Execution and imprisonment threaten their worship, yet they still attend. Meanwhile, lack of sleep, headaches, household chores, the game on TV, weather, and the lake keep us away. In countries hostile to Christianity new believers "sign up" for Christianity knowing the risks, but we don't think it'll ever happen to us. And yet, for some time in America, we've faced nuanced persecution.

After beginning the book with a story of intense persecution, it sounds foolish and almost laughable to read the stories like the one I shared about Jeff and Simone in the previous chapter and to call it persecution. Yet history shows us it's the mild persecution—such as mockery, vilification, prejudice, and marginalization—that has been the most difficult to survive with one's faithfulness intact.

Martyrdom is what we fear the most, but the moment of truth is just that—a moment. With a gun to one's head and asked whether a Christian or not—one only has to be faithful in that moment. Then it's on to glory.

Scripture gives us more teachings to guide us in that situation too. The question, "Do you follow Jesus—yes or no?" presents a clear choice to either remain faithful or to deny Jesus. He said in Matthew 10:33, "Deny me before men I will deny you" (paraphrased). There is no middle ground in that. Yes or no.

It's hard for a professing Christian to make a bold statement of denial, but if there is a situation where middle ground can be used to justify the gray area, then we're tempted to choose the middle ground. In America the line of denying Christ is blurry; therefore we waver much more. As I write this, *Christianity Today* just published a story from Syria, where Christians are being severely persecuted. Many have been killed. The article states that hundreds are in captivity. Just last week 230 Christians were taken from a village. Yet, in all of this, Christianity is growing. Church planters are continuing to start churches.[3] While Islamic militants persecute the Syrian Christians, they continue to witness, and we Americans struggle to witness at all.

Therefore, I'd argue that the scoffing that Jeff may have experienced, and the discrimination that Simone faced, cause more to turn away than the possibility of martyrdom and imprisonment. When we're not being asked point-blank if we believe or not, we find ways to feel as if we are remaining faithful, when we're really just navigating around the persecution. We may not outright deny Christ, but we also try not to go against the grain.

Many Christians in American have bought into the lie that faith is merely a personal thing and therefore is something we keep hidden. We will quickly tell someone about the ball game or movie we watched, but we hardly ever share about our spiritual life. When is the last time someone bragged to you about what they experienced in their personal quiet-time? Christians rarely celebrate God's work in their lives beyond sharing praise requests in church. I have witnessed men who were leaders in churches, and who had strong convictions against using profanity, curse around coworkers so that they would not be seen as weak.

George Barna wrote, "The typical churched believer will die without leading a single person to a lifesaving knowledge of and relationship with Jesus Christ."[4] Much of this is the fear to speak up. Some people who go on short-term mission trips won't tell their friends or coworkers what they are doing for fear of being ridiculed. Regularly Christians sacrifice their convictions against drinking alcohol, having premarital sex, or watching graphic movies so that they won't feel like an outcast or a prude. It shocks me when I talk to singles who have been in long-term dating relationships but talked about their faith with the person they are dating out of fear it might push them away.

The greatest tragedy to the kingdom I have witnessed is when Christians resist the Holy Spirit because of what they feared someone might think. My wife and I just recently wrestled with a decision that was going to cause us to drastically change our lives financially. We were hesitant because of what people would think about our decision. This struggle to obey is not only heightened by the fear of the opinions of friends, but a Christian's decision to obey the Holy Spirit might cost them their job or worse. This fear has kept some from speaking out against laws and actions that are contrary to biblical teaching.

Scoffing is subtle but faith killing. And yet, ever since the "Enlightenment" period in Western history, the supernatural in Scripture has been ridiculed and those who believe in it have been a laughingstock—especially in academia. Like Jeff, Christians who have sought to be scholarly and run in those circles have not been taken seriously; some have even been alienated.

In our universities today, Christian students are regularly ridiculed for their faith and told their beliefs aren't true. Advisers warn them that retaining their Christian values will cost them their careers and acceptance into further education programs. Secular universities have proven to be a dangerous spiritual disaster for Christian students. We must realize this. Statistics and testimonies show that sending our children to college is like sending sheep to the slaughter. A class and professor await them, eager to tell them that God is dead, that we're products of evolution, and that there is no such thing as absolute truth. We warn students more about the "extracurricular" temptations that await them in college, but the greatest danger may be in the classroom.

Unfortunately, higher education isn't the only slaughter-house we send our precious sheep into. Our children first come across those who scoff at biblical teachings and values in public schools. They're being taught a different worldview and different values than we're hoping to instill in them.

We must prepare ourselves and our children for these faith attacks centered on education. Their defense is two-pronged. Our children need to be grounded in Scripture and doctrine, but they must also be walking with God. Often we focus on one or the other. We must do all we can to ensure they know the truth. Yet if we focus on just biblical knowledge, but they don't have an active relationship with God, they'll not withstand the attacks. More often today, we focus only on the relationship and provide a shaky biblical knowledge foundation for our students. We have to do better at teaching Scripture and theology, both at home and at church. The church alone can't do enough. There has to be teaching in the home, but at the same time, the church also has to take its role seriously.

Parents must also take the placement of their children in school and college seriously. They need to be aware of what the school is teaching. They may have to make hard choices. It's especially important that parents focus on the survival of their children's faith when making college choices. You can't put a price tag on your child's faith.

But the classroom isn't the place where we face scoffers. Scoffing at biblical morality also takes place in the public square. Christian values and principles are mocked. We're laughed at and considered old-fashioned. If we speak on behalf of Christian values and against immorality, we're called bigots. Groups such as the ACLU, who have brought lawsuits and moved Christianity out of the public square, have caused us to make the practice of our faith a personal and hidden thing. For the sake of "political correctness," we've shrunk back in our faith. But when we shrink back, other Christians follow suit. Even worse, generations that follow will internalize their faith more and more.

Today, discrimination causes Christians to be excluded from social circles and events. It also impacts believers' careers— preventing advancement or even employment. This is nothing new. Christians have witnessed this type of persecution from the beginning. In Acts, we find the apostles asking Paul to seek donations from other churches in his travels to help the first church in Jerusalem. This collection for the Jerusalem congregation is repeated throughout the Pauline Epistles. Well-known pastor and New Testament commentator John MacArthur writes that overpopulation and famine led to the need, but the need was greater for the Jews who had accepted Christ. He wrote, the plight of these Jewish Christians "were made even more serious" due to persecution. "Many of them were put out of their own homes, stripped of possessions, prevented from getting any but the most menial of jobs, and even imprisoned."[5]

The church in Smyrna was commended for remaining faithful through affliction, poverty, and slander. New Testament scholar Grant Osborne wrote of these three "strengths" Smyrna was commended for possessing. The first affliction should be viewed as persecution and the following two as aspects of that persecution.[6] According to the late Colin Hemer, who was an expert on the seven churches of Asia, poverty was caused by persecution from both Jewish and Hellenistic mobs destroying the property of Christians who were already poor because they would have lost their jobs in that pagan culture.[7] "Poverty has often been the lot of God's followers," wrote Osborne, "because the people of this world hate the children of light and often seek to do them harm."[8]

What makes this persecution so dangerous is that, again, it's part of the daily grind. Even one who initially stands boldly and remains faithful can wear down. One might be faithful one day and struggle the next. It's a struggle to remain faithful when doing so may keep you poor and unemployed. And it's a strain for parents to watch their children become outcasts and maybe not have the "things" their friends have because of a stand for Christ. We are tempted to adjust the "brand" of Christianity we live and not be discriminated against. When you look across the Christian landscape in America, there aren't just different churches or denominations, but there are varying degrees of commitments to following Jesus. Even within denominations of like teachings there are people at different levels in their commitment.

Scripture does not give much room for the legitimacy of these differences. We have passages like Matthew 22:36–37 that instruct us to love the Lord with all of heart, and passages like Matthew 10:37–39 that exhort us to love the Lord in a radical way. Jesus gave His own opinion in Revelation 3:15–16, warning believer not to be lukewarm but to be sold out in our love and faithfulness for Him. Such "extremism" in our love for Christ is the biblical design, but it brings with it ridicule and persecution of scoffing. The temptation is to gravitate to a "brand" of Christianity that allows for a more tolerable way of living.

For a follower of Christ to live a less offensive Christian walk, they have to find ways to deal with the clear scriptural teachings in America. They end up twisting doctrine to accommodate their sinful desires and alleviate persecution. That change of doctrine is unfaithful.

This is far from pleasing to the Lord. Christianity isn't about avoiding the fire. In America we've created whole systems of "Christian" teachings based on avoiding the fires of life or God removing them.

Persecution by scoffing and discrimination has been aimed at Christianity and truth in general for the last several decades—mainly in the form of lawsuits. It has gradually increased. But recently these attacks have become very specific. The push for the legalization of same-sex marriage and gay rights drew a clearer line in the sand. This escalated to the point that on June 26, 2015, same-sex marriage was legalized in every state, despite the church's opposition of it.

Persecution is no longer limited to ridicule and social exclusion; the door for legal persecution is open. The shift poses a great threat to Christians. But the threat isn't the persecution itself. It's not the legal repercussions, nor is it the restraint we face. The real threat is that through these attacks and challenges, Christians might quit practicing their faith or, at the least, accept a lukewarm, middle position and greatly affect the cause of Christ.

For more than two hundred years, we've enjoyed religious liberty in America. These liberties are being challenged. Obamacare called for employers to fund insurance that pays for contraceptives, abortions, and other health measures that violated business owners' religious consciences. For the first time in American history, the state has been able to trump religious liberty.

The legalization of same-sex marriage threatens to violate our religious liberty more. There have already been numerous lawsuits against small businesses that have refused to provide services that would endorse a same-sex union. One of the most notable was the suit filed against a family-owned bakery in Oregon that refused to provide a cake for a same-sex wedding. The lawsuit just topped things off; the baker couple had already lost their business over it. The judge would go even further imposing a gag order that kept the couple from speaking out against the lawsuit.[9]

The Oregon bakery isn't the only marriage service business to be confronted. Multiple florists have been sued. So have rental facilities. A city in Idaho has made it illegal for a pastor to refuse a same-sex couple.[10] We've not even seen the tip of the iceberg yet. Beginning a couple of years before that ruling, and continuing now, I've attended denomination and association meetings on how churches need to protect themselves if they choose to not to perform same-sex marriages. In expectation of lawsuits, church insurance companies are dropping coverage if a church plans to not perform or allow same-sex ceremonies in their facilities.[11]

In Canada, where same-sex marriage has been legal since 2006, preaching against such unions is being called hate speech. The same is occurring in Sweden, who legalized same-sex marriage in 2009 and made it a crime for it to be preached against.[12] Since same-sex marriage has been legalized in the United States, it's only a matter of time before the same is true in the States. Glimpses of this trajectory were beheld when Houston's mayor subpoenaed the sermons of pastors in the city to see if any of them had dared to speak out against homosexuality.[13] The ruling is fresh and the courts are just now beginning to be tested, but evidence of what the future holds can be observed in homosexual activists' push to out U.S. military chaplains who wouldn't conduct same-sex marriages or who preached against it.[14]

Although we blame gay activists, activist judges, or the government, we'll read in the next chapter that demonic deception is behind this loss of religious liberty. Therefore, the endgame isn't merely forbidding Christians to preach against homosexuality, but prohibiting them from preaching and sharing that Jesus is the only way to heaven. The restrictions upon Christians and churches has already caused denominations, churches, and individuals to change their practices and even church doctrine.

It's caused preachers to alter their messages. Others have left the faith because they've flinched at being viewed as a hateful bigot. Others have just backed off on the practice of their faith so they will not have to deal with any lash out.

There are expectations that belonging to churches that continue to speak against homosexuality and same-sex marriage will eventually cause employees to be terminated or prevent someone from being hired. This has already been the case in many situations. In 2014, the Atlanta fire chief was fired for speaking out against homosexuality a book he wrote for the men's Bible study group in his local church. It wasn't something he did on the job; he had simply included it in his curriculum.[15]

In April 2016 a Missouri State University student was expelled from the university's counseling program because of his acceptance of traditional marriage. The expulsion after he shared concerns about his own willingness to counsel same-sex couples.[16]

As this discrimination increases, we're going to be tempted to abandon our faith or suppress it internally, therefore not practicing it, so our employment and income won't be affected. We must realize that to shrink back in our faith due to a job loss or ridicule isn't any different from recanting our faith while we eye the end of a gun barrel.

My fear is that we'll handle increased scrutiny of our faith by keeping our faith to ourselves. A "teaching" on and trend toward keeping one's Christianity internal already exists. We have to view suppressing our faith as denying Christ, as Peter did.

It's not just the ridicule or discrimination that threatens our faith. Right now, while you read this book, you have an enemy who wishes to kill you because you're a Christian. We watch the horrific persecution of Iraqi Christians by ISIS and other

Islamic terrorist groups on the news, but those same terrorists want our heads even more than the ones they're chopping off now. Your name and picture is on their wanted poster. They want you dead. They hate you. For the time being they're kept at bay across the ocean. We appear to be protected, but just as the Romans wanted Christians eradicated in its early history, you and I are wanted dead.

We must also be aware of how fast things can change. In 2015, a tragic shooting in a Charleston, South Carolina, church ignited a spark that lit a national powder keg. Instantly across the nation the Confederate flag became the sacrificial lamb. Stores pulled items off the shelves if they contained or displayed images of the flag. State capitols took the flags down. Even flags at Civil War battlefields were brought down. This took place in a matter of weeks.

Nineteen hundred years ago a similar swift reaction occurred in the Roman Empire. A large fire engulfed much of Rome, and Christians were blamed. They became the sacrificial lambs. Immediately a powder keg of persecution was lit against Christians. They were fiercely killed. With the table already being tipped against Christianity it's not going to take much to quickly change and for the intolerance to escalate.

The discussion of persecution to this point has centered on how we're affected personally, but our faith is in danger when our loved ones are persecuted or are threatened with persecution. I know this is what I struggle with the most. If it were only about me facing persecution, I don't think I'd have an ounce of fear. However, knowing my daughters are going to be persecuted makes me struggle. This is the area where I need to prepare the most.

In the story of the Iraqi family in chapter 1, the husband and wife had talked through the effect that persecution would have on their children. This is vital. American families are already struggling with their children being persecuted for their faith. In February 2015, American parents received word that their daughter, Kayla Mueller, had been killed. She'd been taken hostage in Syria while carrying out mission work there. In June they were informed that Kayla had been kept for a sex slave by the emir of the Islamic State.[17]

ISIS and other groups that are hell-bent on slaughtering the Christian "infidels" long to kill our sons and rape our daughters. Right now, as you read this, if they could get their hands on them, they would. This is more terrifying than losing my own life. The fear of our children suffering tempts us to suppress or retreat in our faith. Kayla recognized the interconnectivity persecution has on families, as she was more concerned about her parents' suffering than her own.[18]

As parents and loved ones of those who may be persecuted, we need to realize their faithfulness and our faithfulness on their behalf is of the greatest importance. The confidence in God Kayla revealed in her final letter should give her parents great joy. Knowing that persecution is prophesied should help us cope as parents. These prophecies should also encourage us to remain faithful.

## THE COMING PERSECUTION

The prophecy of Matthew 24:9–10 is a template to the challenges we Christians will go up against until Jesus returns, but it particularly tells of one specific time period. Jesus' words in this passage follow the disciples' question regarding what signs would precede His return. Jesus told them that, in addition to a great falling away, persecution would occur simultaneously in every place in the world where Christians are located. This persecution will be the most intense and universal in history. We don't know exactly when this will transpire, but it's coming. The world is moving toward this event.

In this final persecution, we know from the book of Revelation, many will be martyred (see Rev. 6:9–11). A Christian who remains faithful won't even be able to buy food (13:16–18). Remaining faithful in this persecution will be the greatest challenge to ever befall Christianity. Yet over and over again the book of Revelation promises rewards for those who do remain faithful, such as a crown of life (Rev. 2:10) and sitting on the throne with Christ (Rev. 2:10).

So if the United States remains a nation to the end, persecution will break out here. The descriptions of the coming persecution are horrible, but what I can't emphasize enough is that what we should fear the most is that the persecution will break our faith.

We need to know persecution can cause us to turn away. Peter thought it would not happen to him. When he was warned, he blew off Jesus' words and boldly stated he'd never falter. Peter would have been wise to realize Jesus' words were true even for him. We would also do well to realize Jesus' words are for us. It's easy to read prophecies about persecution causing the abandoning of faith and feel we're immune, but we're not. Therefore, we must prepare.

Persecution is scary and powerful, but we're equipped to stand strong.

One could argue that Peter did not yet have the Holy

Spirit when he denied Jesus. However, every other time Peter experienced persecution, the Holy Spirit dwelled in him, and he did not fail. It was the empowerment of the Spirit made the difference.

So we should take comfort in the knowledge that we have the Holy Spirit, but we must also be filled with Him and walking with Him. Therefore, since we have the power indwelling in us, we must make walking in the Spirit our priority.

# SPIRITUAL PREPPER'S CHECKLIST

In the next chapter, we will look beyond the curtain at the forces behind the hatred of Christians, and it will become even more apparent that being filled with the Spirit is the key. In that chapter we will look more in-depth at walking in the Spirit. The imminent threat of persecution calls for specific items for preparation.

☐ Stay aware of the persecution around the world.

As mentioned in the last chapter praying for ministries like the Voice of the Martyrs, Open Doors USA, and International Christian Concern is good. Also consider supporting missionaries around the world. Read their updates and pray for them. When our hearts are set on caring for our fellow Christians all over the globe, persecution begins to be more real to our everyday life.

☐ Pledge allegiance to Jesus not a church program.

Although the threat of martyrdom may be a long way from the shores of the United States, attacks on religious liberty and possibly the tax-exempt status of churches ensure Christian churches in America will change. It might mean the end of big programs and organized events. We need the fellowship, encouragement, relationship, and training we receive through a church, but we don't necessarily have to have the programs. It is important to be connected to small groups and practice organic evangelism through relationships. Even if church life changes in America our faith needs to live on.

☐ Prioritize security in your church.

Fortunately, church security is no longer taboo. Recent church violence has caused leaders to consider it. As a pastor or church leader you have a responsibility to keep your people safe. There are great resources out there. Strategos International has been a leader in this ministry. Sheepdog Seminars and Brotherhood Mutual Insurance are great resources as well.

As a church member, security has to become a real life concern for your worship experience. We have to wake up and take this need seriously.

# 5

# PREPPING FOR FIERY DARTS

. . . taking the shield of faith with which you will be able to quench all the fiery darts of the wicked one.

—EPHESIANS 6:16 (NKJV)

## A STRATEGICALLY TIMED SPIRITUAL DISASTER

Ryan became a Christian at a large, citywide revival. Then a mutual friend recommended our church to him. From the first day I met him and through our three months of daily interaction, I was blown away by Ryan's zeal and his boldness.

I was double-checking my video presentation before the worship service when Ryan came into our church for the first time. He didn't waste any time sharing his testimony with me. Although Ryan was in his midtwenties, he'd never heard the gospel or been in church. Someone had convinced him to attend that revival to hear the band, and that night his life drastically changed.

A week later I baptized him, and spent hours with him afterwards teaching him what it meant to follow Jesus. I'm not sure I've ever met someone who dove wholeheartedly into their Christian walk so fast. Every time you saw Ryan, he bubbled over with an incredible peace and infectious happiness. He was as on fire as anyone I've seen. He never missed a worship service. He was involved in everything—Bible studies, the property maintenance ministry, children's ministry, student ministry, and sound-tech ministry. Ryan took me to more than a dozen of his family's and friends' homes to share the gospel.

Everything in his life transformed, not just on the inside. He completely changed his wardrobe. Every time I saw him, he had on a different Christian T-shirt. He had an armful of bracelets with Christian sayings on them: WWJD (What Would Jesus Do?), FROG (Fully Relying on God). You name it, he had it. He wore a cross necklace. Christian bumper stickers covered his truck. His radio was set on Christian radio, and he gave me a good run on the number of Christian concerts he'd attended.

Ryan was the man on fire—but in three months Ryan was gone. Now, a couple of years later, Ryan has not been back or even returned calls from me or his Christian friends. I assume he's alive. I've literally checked obituaries numerous times. I did get behind his truck one time; the bumper stickers were gone. I lost him when I tried to trail him.

I'm not sure what happened. Its possible several things came up and discouraged him. Whatever the particular event was, it caused him to turn away. He's no longer practicing his faith.

Already, as we've looked at cases of individuals turning from the practice of their faith, we identified the particular spiritual disaster that hit each of them. The disaster itself isn't the only detail that needs to be identified; so does the timing. A challenge to the faith can be greatly enhanced by its timing. This was the case for Ryan. The discouragement he faced came early in his Christian walk, as if it had been strategically placed to derail his faith and prevent him from continuing on.

I wish I knew what exactly happened in Ryan's life. My guess is he encountered the scoffing type of persecution Simone faced in chapter 2, or he just got busy. I know he had taken a new job with crazy shifts. He may have just lost the habit of churchgoing, and that bled over to the rest of his life. I'm not sure, but it's heartbreaking.

## THE AFTERMATH

In Ryan's three short months at our church, he brought a freshness and fire that rekindled and rejuvenated the church. He had reinforced my own personal confidence in the power of the gospel and had motivated my evangelistic efforts. When he disappeared, I was left discouraged. In full disclosure, it made me a little gun-shy in my witnessing. Ryan's disappearance didn't only affect me, but disheartened our whole church.

Ryan had such potential to be used to share Christ with others, but we may never get to witness what God could have done through him. The children in his small group were devestated. For months, they asked when he was coming back. The youth small group he assisted felt the same way. Though he'd also initiated some great changes to the production of our worship service, all of the measures he'd worked hard to implement were left undone.

I followed up on several of those family members and friends Ryan had introduced me to on our evangelistic visits. Some of them had initially been open to the gospel, but Ryan's turning away had pushed them away too.

To this day I'm skeptical every time a new Christian jumps into his or her faith with a zeal and boldness like Ryan's. It's a shame, but again, our faith failures in spiritual disasters don't only affect us, but others—those immediately around us and others whom we haven't even met. I hold out hope that whatever happened, this won't be Ryan's spiritual doomsday.

Ryan's saga has caused some who know him to question the validity of his salvation. It's hard for me to argue with the evidential joy he displayed, but I'm still miffed by what occurred. Jesus' parable of the sower rings in my head (see Matt. 13).

Did the seed of the gospel sown into Ryan's heart really land on rocky ground? Did "birds" snatch the seed up? Did "thorns" strangle the seed out? Is it true salvation if it doesn't "take"? Or will Ryan produce fruit at a later point because he was truly born again?

I'm not sure, but I'd not want to live with those questions being asked of my own life.

### FORECASTED, STRATEGIC TRAPS AND ATTACKS

While I don't know what happened to Ryan, I do know it was a perfectly timed trap. It wasn't just coincidence. It was the handiwork of the enemies of all Christians—Satan and his demonic forces. Spiritual disasters may seem to simply rise naturally out of life, but a forgotten prophecy in 1 Timothy 4 peels back a spiritual disaster to expose its inner workings. The prophecy reveals that spiritual disasters aren't coincidental, but are deceptive traps employed by our enemy.

The apostle Paul gives us this insight:

> The Spirit clearly says that in later times some will abandon the faith and follow deceiving spirits and things taught by demons. Such teachings come through hypocritical liars, whose consciences have been seared as with a hot iron. (1 Tim. 4:1–2)

Paul was speaking specifically about false doctrine, which is a dangerous and a threatening spiritual disaster that I'll address more in chapter 9.

This forgotten prophecy in 1 Timothy begins by warning that, as this age ends, professed Christians will leave the faith—or at least the practice of their faith—and embrace instead demonic philosophies. If one only read this first verse, it would appear this was just another prophecy on false teaching. It would be easy to see the references to deceiving spirits and demons as only figurative language, but verse 2 reveals what's actually going on in the false teacher's heart and mind. Paul wrote that false teaching comes from individuals who have had their consciences seared by repeated sin. Their hearts have become hardened, and, desiring to continue in their sin, they alter their teaching to suit their own sinful desires. Second Timothy 4:3–4 goes on to say that people will flock to these teachers "to suit their desires." Finally, Paul pulled back all the layers and taught us that it is Satan and his demons who initiate the false teaching. They are the architects behind the spiritual disaster of these doctrines. Based on this passage and Matthew 24:9–10, then, it is reasonable to state that all spiritual disasters—persecution, temptation, difficult trials, false teaching, and so on—are orchestrated by our enemy.

When someone desires to persecute a Christian, he, like the false teacher, is also motivated by his sinful desires. That may spring from a personal hatred of Christ, jealousy, anger, or a list of things. The persecutor continues and follows through with persecution because his heart has become calloused and his conscience seared. The persecutor is still to blame, but behind the act, behind the persecutor, behind the evil desire that motivates him, and behind the calloused heart that causes him to follow through are evil spiritual forces that desire to wear down the persecuted Christian.

This means there is both a strategy and a sinister purpose to spiritual disasters. The destruction of your faith and the corresponding domino effect on the kingdom of Christ is that purpose.

In another epistle, the apostle Paul again peels back the outer layer of the challenges to our faith. In Ephesians 6, he gives us an important warning that has great significance in our preparation for our spiritual doomsday. Paul wrote:

> Put on the full armor of God so that you can take your stand against the devil's schemes. For our struggle is not against flesh and blood, but against the rulers, against the authorities, against the powers of this dark world and against the spiritual forces of evil in the heavenly realms. Therefore put on the full armor of God, so that when the day of evil comes, you may be able to stand your ground, and after you have done everything, to stand. Stand firm then, with the belt of truth buckled around your waist, with the breastplate of righteousness in place, and with your feet fitted with the readiness that comes from the gospel of peace. In addition to all this, take up the shield of faith, with which you can extinguish all the

flaming arrows of the evil one. Take the helmet of salvation and the sword of the Spirit, which is the word of God. And pray in the Spirit on all occasions with all kinds of prayers and requests. With this in mind, be alert and always keep on praying for all the saints. (vv. 11–18)

This passage and the one in 1 Timothy reveal that we're at war—a spiritual war. Each spiritual disaster we face is a flaming arrow or fiery dart from our adversary. But this passage gives us a "checklist" for spiritual prepping. Followers of Christ are told to beware because they could be attacked in the areas of truth, righteousness, evangelism, and faith. Therefore, each of us need to prepare accordingly by arming ourselves with God's Word and fervent prayer.

I wish I could say *Spiritual Prepper* was the first of its kind, but biblical teachers and Christian leaders have been urging believers to prepare for faith-wrecking disasters throughout Christian history. One of the most famous spiritual doomsday prepping books was written in 1678 by a preacher who faced a trial of persecution himself. John Bunyan wrote the classic *Pilgrim's Progress* while in prison for preaching what had been outlawed. Bunyan's work tells the story of a man named Christian and his journey through life. Christian's goal was to stay on the narrow path and remain faithful to God throughout his journey. He sought to hear "Well done, My good and faithful servant" when he entered the gate of the Eternal City. Christian is symbolic of all Christians, and the journey is symbolic of the life of a follower of Christ.

Christian's journey led him to a narrow gate through which he had to pass to find life and to remain faithful. When he approached the gate, a gatekeeper abruptly pulled him inside. This left Christian very startled by the bold move. The gate-keeper said, "A short distance from this Gate stands a strong castle of which Beelzebub is their ruler. From there, both he and those with him shoot arrows at those who come up to this Gate, hoping they'll die before they can enter in."[1]

Later in Christian's journey, a "disgusting fiend" named Apollyon "straddled over the whole breadth of the Path" and "shot a flaming arrow at Christian's chest." Apollyon sought to prevent Christian from remaining faithful in his journey. He wanted Christian to turn away. As Christian fought back against the fiery arrows, "Apollyon charged him, shooting arrows as thick as hail."[2] Of course, we all know that it was really Satan and his demons who were so hell-bent on shooting those fiery darts to keep Christian from remaining faithful and to cause him to turn away.

This imagery isn't isolated to only Bunyan's story, but it's the reality found in Scripture. We read in Ephesians 6 how Satan and his forces wage war against us. More insight is given in 1 Peter 5:8, which describes Satan as a roaring lion seeking to devour us and our faith. And the apostle John wrote , "The thief comes only to steal and kill and destroy; [but Jesus came] that [we] may have life, and have it to the full" (John 10:10). Satan is the thief. He's out to destroy the life we have in Christ. He wants to crush *your* faith.

You and I are wanted men and women. Our face and names are on the poster. And Satan and his minons are the posse; they seek to derail our faith.

In high school football we ran a drill called "the gauntlet." There would be two lines made by everyone on the team. The two lines faced each other and stood so that players on one side could reach out and touch the fingertips of the players on the other. Then one by one we each tucked the ball to our chest with both hands and ran through the gauntlet. Every player in the two lines swatted and ripped trying to knock the ball loose. There was a fury of swinging arms. If you survived to the end with the ball, your arms were red and numb.

That's the Christian life. As Christians, we run through the "gauntlet" of life clenching our faith while demon-driven trials seek to rip our faith away.

## SERIOUSLY, DEMONS

I can hear critics right now saying, "Here is another Christian saying there is a demon or devil under every rock."

That's not what I'm saying. This isn't fearmongering. This is the truth.

Though they may not be under every rock, Scripture teaches us that they're behind our spiritual disasters.

Although the hatred of Christians drives the Islamic jihadist to persecute and execute Christians, the reality is that the deceptive work of demons are pushing the jihadist to do it. In America we blame liberals, the media, or groups such as the ACLU for attacking our religious liberties, and they are, but behind that push is demonic activity. Behind the religious liberty–destroying political correctness of America is the work of a spiritual enemy. Behind the push for redefining marriage and gender isn't merely the activists but Satan himself. The same is true for all the challenges we face.

Fiery darts are being launched at us, and those darts threaten to push us away from our faith.

WELL-TIMED TRAPS

One of the scenes in *Pilgrim's Progress* that captures the strategic trappings of the enemy is at the beginning of Christian's journey. Immediately after deciding to follow Christ, he faces the Slough of Despondency. Like my friend Ryan, Christian takes off on his journey boldly and with great excitement. If this story were written today, Christian would have covered the back of his vehicle with bumper stickers and that silver fish. He would have locked his radio in on K-Love, like Ryan. Immediately Christian fell into a miry and frustrating swamp. Fighting through the quicksand quickly tempered his excitement. Christian persevered, but his fellow pilgrim, Pliable, gave up and turned away. Pliable's faith had been destroyed. Although almost four hundred years earlier, Bunyan accurately allegorized Ryan's turning from the faith.

In C. S. Lewis's 1942 masterpiece, *The Screwtape Letters*, Lewis captured the role of demons in derailing the faith of Christians. The book presents the dialogue of two fictional demons—an older demon and his younger nephew. The older demon mentors the younger on how to deceive their human target, and in one of their correspondences, he tells him not to fret if the human becomes a Christian because many have turned away from Christ in the beginning of their walk. Lewis, writing from the viewpoint of Uncle Screwtape, says:

> I note with grave displeasure that your patient has become a Christian. Do not indulge the hope that you will escape the usual penalties; indeed, in your better moments, I trust you would hardly even wish to do so. In the meantime we must make the best of the situation. There is no need to despair; hundreds of these adult converts have been reclaimed after a

brief sojourn in the Enemy's camp and are now with us. All the habits of the patient, both mental and bodily, are still in our favour.[3]

The two famous works of Bunyan and Lewis capture how our enemy targets us with spiritual disasters at the start of our walk, but that's only *one* example of a strategically placed faith trap. The prowling enemy looks for the perfect times to challenge our faith. There are times when we're more susceptible than others. His timing could come on the heels of a great spiritual high or victory, when our guard is dropped, or when we're under lots of stress. Rarely is there only one fiery dart shot at one time. They tend to come in clusters. We may dodge the initial arrow, but the next one strikes us. With so many fiery darts, we face the temptation of growing weary and being struck.

Knowing demons are behind the potential faith wreckers we face should push us to make our preparations spiritually because the battle is spiritual. It should also challenge us to examine our weaknesses. It's in the chinks in our armor that the enemy will attack. It's when we're unarmed or sleeping that he sneaks in to plunder.

Satan will shoot fiery darts at you. He's shooting them now. They could be in the form of any spiritual disaster, but you can bet they'll be at significant times in your Christian walk.

Peter's denial of Jesus serves as our precedent for identifying the nature and effects of spiritual disasters in our lives. We've read that the fear of persecution led to a spiritual disaster for Peter. Specifically, when he watched Jesus be arrested and realized he'd be next.

The surface culprit for that faith-wrecking disaster were

the soldiers who actually captured Jesus. If we look further, the cause originated with the Jewish leadership that hated Jesus and wanted Him killed. But even deeper into the anatomy of Peter's spiritual disaster is where we find the real culprit—Satan. He was behind Jesus' arrest and crucifixion. Satan's involvement was the fulfillment of Genesis 3:15, which predicted that Satan would "strike [H]is heel." The arrest, beating, and cross was Satan's heel biting. Jesus made even further revelations about the satanic foundation of Peter's dilemma in Luke, where Jesus says, "Simon, Simon, Satan has asked to sift . . . you as wheat. But I have prayed for you, Simon, that your faith may not fail. And when you have turned back, strengthen your brothers."[4]

Satan wants to sift you and me as he did Peter.

## A DIRTY ENEMY

Although the United States greatly outpowered the Vietcong during the Vietnam War, the Vietcong were difficult to defeat because they didn't step out onto the battlefield and fight conventionally. They fought a guerrilla war. Guerrilla warfare is irregular or unconventional warfare. The Vietcong used tunnels, underground hidden bases, and they fought few open battles. They mainly ambushed American forces, set traps, used suicide bombers, and fought a war of attrition to slowly degrade our army. The North Vietnamese had borrowed a page from the United States of America's own history book.

Much credit has been given to some of the unconventional techniques used by the Continental Army during the American Revolution. George Washington led the Continental Army in a convincing victory when he surprised the British by crossing the Delaware River on Christmas night. General Marion Francis became famous and was nicknamed the "Swamp Fox" because of his victorious guerrilla warfare during that same war.

Guerrilla warfare is just one example of unconventional warfare. Throughout history shrewd generals have conceived many unconventional strategies to gain victory. There have been deceptive maneuvers and blind-siding ambushes. During World War II, while the Allied Forces prepared for the D-Day invasion on the French shores, they deceived the Germans by creating an entire inflatable Ghost Army staged in England. Propaganda campaigns have also been used with great success to intimidate or deceive an opposing army.

Satan is an unconventional general. Our enemies in this spiritual war are guerrilla fighters—they're spiritual terrorists. Satan's guerrilla nature is revealed in Ephesian 6:11, where we're warned to stand against "the devil's schemes." We aren't warned to stand against his great strength or his superior forces—he has to find ways to compensate for being the weaker force. His army is outnumbered by the heavenly angelic army two to one (see Rev. 12:3–4). He's also fighting the Almighty. The spoils of war he offers us are as empty as the inflatable tanks the Allied forces used to dupe German intelligence in World War II. To cover Satan's own shortcomings and the shortcomings of his army, the demonic forces must employ deception.

In Ephesians 6:14 we're told to stand firm against false teaching with the "belt of truth." Knowing the truth is vital for spiritual prepping because our enemy, the "thief" of John 10:10, seeks to take the blessings we have in Christ. In a closely related passage, Satan's servants, the false prophets, are referred to as wolves in sheep's clothing (Matt. 7:15).

Scripture presents a clear case showing that Satan fights this war with deception. We find him in the opening pages of the text and human history as a serpent deceiving Adam and Eve (see Gen. 3). Satan is using the same deceptive craftiness against us today. In 2 Corinthians 11, Paul warned the Corinthian Christians, "I'm afraid that, as the serpent deceived Eve by his craftiness, your minds will be led astray from the simplicity and purity of devotion to Christ . . . and no wonder, for Satan himself masquerades as an angel of light" (v. 3 NASB, v. 14). Jesus made it clear during his ministry on earth that Satan was a deceiver: "He was a murderer from the beginning, not holding to the truth, for there is no truth in him. When he lies, he speaks his native language, for he is a liar and the father of lies" (Matt. 8:44).

Every spiritual disaster we'll face is an attack from the enemy. His goal is the destruction of our faith, and in each attack we can expect some type of deception. In the meantime, Jesus described our faithful relationship with Him as a great treasure worthy of us selling off everything to possess: "The kingdom of heaven is like treasure hidden in a field. When a man found it, he hid it again, and then in his joy went and sold all he had and bought that field" (Matt. 13:44). If you've trusted Jesus as your Savior and have begun that relationship with Him, then you know this is absolutely true. You've felt it. You've experienced it. I know I have. Satan's deceptive disasters are simply attempts to make us forget how great the treasure of Christ truly is in our life. We must remember we're in a spiritual fight and that we're fighting a deceiver.

We're also fighting in his territory.

## LIVING IN THE ENEMY'S TERRITORY

In this spiritual war, we Christians are always the away team. This world belongs to the enemy, so we're fighting in enemy territory. This is vital for us to comprehend. We're even more susceptible to failing an attack on our faith because we're in his territory.

I don't want to give Satan more credit than he deserves. Yes, God owns this world, but He's allowed Satan to be the prince of this present age and world. Over and over again Scripture warns us that just as Satan is an enemy to our faith, so is this world. It's hard to precisely define "the world." We must view this world as an extension of Satan and the demonic forces' deceptive campaign. They've had at least six thousand years to cover this world with traps and propaganda to catch us at our every move. The world around us has been molded to devastate our faith. For there to be an environment to strengthen and increase our faith, we have to create it or seek it out.

As we move ahead and reflect on the possible challenges to our faith—look deeper. When we look deeper, we realize our real enemy and the real purpose of spiritual disaster. With each challenge we discuss, it'll get worst. As we draw closer to the end, the evil spiritual forces will be less restrained.

# SPIRITUAL PREPPER'S CHECKLIST

This chapter got to the central cause of spiritual disasters—a spiritual war. Therefore, to fight this good fight, we must prepare strategically and spiritually.

☐ Think strategically in your spiritual life.

Hopefully by this point you have been convinced to protect your faithfulness. We have to realize we are in a war, and our faith can be a casualty. The chapter opened with Ryan facing a spiritual disaster at a point when he was weak. The enemy is strategic so we must be too. This requires you to think ahead. If you are at a weak point, rely on your accountability partner or small group. Seek help when you are down. Be on guard following successes. Don't just approach your walk with Christ haphazardly.

☐ Be filled with the Spirit.

In the last chapter I shared that the key to Peter's success in his spiritual battles was the possession of the Holy Spirit. If you have trusted Christ, you have received His Spirit as a guide in your life, but simply possessing Him is not enough. In Ephesians 5:18, we're instructed to be filled with the Holy Spirit rather than wine. We never "get" more of the Holy Spirit, when we received him into our lives we "got" all of Him. This passage speaks more to influence. Like how alcohol can influence our thoughts, words, and actions so should the Spirit. The more of our lives He impacts and influences the better. Famous pastor James Montgomery Boice wrote, "[being filled with Holy Spirit] refers to our being so under the Holy Spirit's control and leading that our thought and life are entirely taken up with Jesus Christ."[5]

In preparation for these attacks on our spiritual lives we must walk in step with the Spirit, which means leaving sin. It takes a regular meeting with God—a quiet time. It takes being in His Word and prayer. There are so many great resources on prayer, but Mark Batterson's *Draw the Circle: The 40 Day Prayer Challenge* revolutionized my prayer life. Or read Henry Blackaby's *Experiencing God*, Mark Batterson's *Wild Goose Chase*, and Charles Stanley's *The Spirit Filled Life*. I encourage you to keep a prayer journal. Seek the Lord wholeheartedly, and He will reveal himself.

☐ Pray.

As far as effectiveness, this is the number one way we accomplish anything in life. Simply effectively praying can bring the needed strength, endurance, and perseverance. Prayer is not the last resort but is the first skill we need to master in order to be prepared.

# 6

# PREPPING IN A WEAKENED CHURCH

"At that time many will turn away from the faith . . . The love of most will grow cold."

—MATTHEW 24:10, 12

## AN UNNECESSARY SPIRITUAL DISASTER

The Sunday before her high school graduation, Camille walked across the stage of one of the leading churches in the world's largest denomination to receive a commemorative Bible. She laughed with her friends when she saw herself in pictures in the graduation slide show. There were pictures of her at the laser tag trip, the water park lock-in, the amusement park, a major league baseball game, the annual ski trip, and the one time the student ministry hosted a square dance. The night before, at the senior dinner, when the microphone was handed to her for her to share a testimony or a memory, she said that the ski trips were always her favorite. She then shared how a little girl in a backyard Bible club at the one mission trip she went on had touched her life. She'd learned to always help people because of that little girl.

That same Bible she received at graduation sits today on a shelf in her entertainment center. It's as crisp and clean as it was the day she received it. Her son asked her about it just the other day. It's amazing what good shape the Bible is in after multiple moves from different dorms, her college apartment, and now their second home since getting married.

Camille was raised in church—a large, famous church known for its missions giving and annual Bible conference. Her parents only attended on Sunday mornings for worship, but they made sure Camille participated in the children's choir and all the special singing programs. They had her there for every vacation Bible school and for fun children's events. Camille attended children's church on Sunday mornings, but the family never made Sunday school a priority. After she reached teenage years, Camille's parents let her make her own decision about attending. She occasionally went to Sunday worship services. She made only a few student worship services, but all of the trips and activities—even one mission trip—and she did make a profession of faith at vacation Bible school. She said she loved Jesus and professed to be a Christian.

Following graduation Camille went to college. She loved college. She met great friends, got very involved, and joined a sorority her first year. On her first few visits back home, she attended worship with her parents. But on following visits she'd sleep in while her parents went to worship. By the end of her first year, her parents had stopped attending church. They'd accomplished their Christian task. They had "raised" Camille in church—a good church, too.

Camille never stepped in church again. Her wedding was a destination wedding. The couple didn't even contact her old youth pastor or any other pastor. Her husband had a fraternity buddy who got licensed online to officiate the wedding.

She still professed to be a Christian, but remained out of church until her son was old enough to participate in children's programs. Camille then picked the church that offered the most activities. Like her parents, she attended only on Sunday mornings but made sure her child was involved in everything. But unlike her parents, Camille attended alone. Her husband knew nothing about church. Christ has little influence on Camille's life.

It's hard to even call what derailed Camille's spiritual life a spiritual disaster. A disaster constitutes something big or difficult, which wasn't the case with Camille. Maybe it was busyness. Maybe it was peer pressure or scoffing from friends—more accurately, it could've been the anticipation of their scoffing. Maybe it was materialism or the pursuit of status or reputation. To some extent it was sin, but Camille never went completely off the deep end. She maintained some type of conscience although she never articulated it herself.

Some might even say Camille is practicing her faith—she attends church and she makes sure her son attends. She helps out as a sponsor on church trips, but as I've stressed, church isn't the epitome of our faith. Camille doesn't pray. She hasn't read her Bible since that tenth grade mission trip. She's never shared her faith. She's never grown in her faith. In reality, it appears Camille doesn't have a relationship with Jesus.

Camille is one of the statistical 20 percent who were raised in church and continue to be engaged with it.[1] Although she's still engaged with church and Christianity, her faith is lukewarm. It took little to nothing to "wreck" her faith. The issue is, Camille grew up in a weakened church, which made her vulnerable to spiritual disasters. The complacency of her parents and her church's culture left her unprepared to live out her faith. From the outside looking in and even as a member, the church did not look weak. Rather it was a leader in her denomination. It was respected nationally as a leading church, but even some of the best churches in America are producing weak Christ followers, and they just don't know it. Overall Christianity in America is weak compared to other parts of the world and other points of history.

## THE EFFECTS OF A WEAKENED CHURCH

It may be difficult to clearly define what exactly has kept Camille from living wholeheartedly for the Lord, but it's easy to recognize the effects on her life and others due to her complacent Christianity.

In the prophecies of Revelation 2 and 3 we find warnings against complacency. The church of Ephesus was told they were serving without passion for Jesus (see 2:2, 4). Laodicea was called "lukewarm" in their relationship with Christ (3:16). Sardis was called dead (3:1). One church was warned of losing their "lampstand" (2:5). The temple's menorah is believed to be the intended symbol. It was used to light the way to the Holy of Holies—the way to God.[2]

The lampstand is representative of our witness and the personal blessings that come from walking with God. Camille, like the churches in Sardis and Laodicea, was void of the lampstand. It wasn't removed, but rather, suppressed. Camille was robbed of what she could have had in Jesus. She never experienced the blessings she could have, but only tasted those briefly on that one short-term mission trip. She also never shined her light to guide others. Throughout her life she never witnessed to any of her friends in high school, college, or in the sphere of her life now. She never witnessed to other family members. There have been countless lost strangers that have walked into her life and walked out still lost.

She turned down mission trip opportunities and countless volunteer opportunities. She's only *taken* from the church and missed the many opportunities to give back or to encourage and bless others.

Dangerously, Camille was away from the influence of church and Scripture when she made the biggest decisions of her life. She chose her college, college major, career, friends, and husband on her own without seeking direction from the Lord. Chances are she doesn't even know the Holy Spirit she possesses would have directed her steps. Even though she desires for her son to go to church, his maturation in Christ is going to be difficult since his father isn't a Christian. Unless something changes in Camille's spiritual life, her son will follow her pattern of spirituality. Camille's husband may never hear the gospel himself.

## MORE SPIRITUAL DISASTERS DUE TO A
## WEAKENED CHURCH

Marcus became sold-out for God his sophomore year of high school. During a youth crusade God moved in his life in a powerful way. He had grown up in church—there every time the door was open. He went to Sunday school, children's church, after-school children's programs, Bible drill, youth group, and Fellowship of Christian Athletes (FCA) gatherings, and went on every mission trip he could.

Immediately after that youth crusade, Marcus began making a huge impact in his high school and in his youth group. He learned to play the guitar and led worship at his youth group and local youth events. He gave devotions for his student ministry and at FCA meetings. He absolutely loved to worship.

During his senior year he committed his life to vocational ministry. That next fall he attended a state university, but in keeping his vow to God about ministry, he majored in religion. His fire for God followed him to the university. Marcus witnessed to everyone he saw. He volunteered at a local church and a local Young Life chapter. He led worship at a campus ministry.

In his second year at college, Marcus entered his religion classes and encountered many things he'd never considered—he didn't realize the secular slant of the teaching he would receive. After his first course, he was convinced the Bible wasn't "inspired." It contained too many inaccuracies. Class after class eroded his faith. Eventually he quit all of his ministry work and dropped out of church. His Christian concert trips turned into late nights of drinking at a bar. He changed his major to philosophy and considered himself an atheist. He no longer believed God created the world. He thought Jesus was just a historical figure who taught about a better life.

Marcus's childhood church was a great church. I don't know if you could find a place where the worship was more exciting or more passionate. Marcus went to everything offered to him. He was prepared to have enthusiasm for God and to serve Him, but a weakened church hadn't prepared him to combat the false teaching and the intense ridicule from professors he encountered in college. They had not prepared him for *spiritual disaster*. You see, his exciting and passionate childhood church had focused on experience, not doctrine.

There was great spiritual fallout in Marcus's life. The good things he was doing and the impact he had on others ceased. The worst aftermath from his faith failure is that he will now further perpetrate the fallacies that a weakened church had not prepared him to encounter.

## A FALSELY SWOLLEN CHURCH

This morning while I drove to the office, I listened to American Family Radio's Dan Celia. I don't understand economic numbers very well, but Dan was sharing the year's second quarter statistics. He was explaining how the government's predictive numbers for inflation looked better than reality because they exclude food and energy costs from the statistics. If food and energy were included, the numbers would reveal a greater inflation. He further explained that the statistics looked better than reality because the government used a smaller population number. He insisted the numbers weren't true numbers.

I believe we experience the same type of faulty perception regarding the American church. Although statistics of church attendance aren't fantastic, they are much better than the reality of faithfulness. The American church has been swollen in attendance, but that attendance doesn't equal faithfulness to the Lord. This isn't the situation in other nations or at other points of history, but it's not something unanticipated, as Matthew 24 implies this phenomenon. In verse 10, we read that *many* will turn from the faith. For there to be a *many,* the church must grow large.

This exponential growth in the church in America was a false swelling. When extra growth occurred, it would be celebrated as great success. It would be glory days for the church.

Although the Bible promises success in the spreading of the gospel, Scripture also tells over and over that those who travel *the* narrow path will be few. So during times when churches have great success and have grown to comprise the majority of a nation's population, unfaithfulness will be found in its ranks.

David Kinnamon, a researcher and author with the Barna Group, did not hold back when he addressed the swollen church in America, "Christianity has become bloated with blind followers who would rather repeat slogans than actually feel true compassion and care. Christianity has become marketed and streamlined into a juggernaut of fear-mongering that has lost its own heart."[3]

The false growth of today includes those who haven't truly been saved, but it also includes those who may truly be saved but aren't living faithfully. The false growth that has resulted in our large churches today includes not only those who are not living faithfully, but also those who are not saved at all. Matthew 13:24–43 points to this event. The passage is familiarly called the parable of wheat and tares or in the NIV, the Parable of Weeds. In it, Jesus explained that the "weeds" will look identical to the wheat and will grow along with the wheat. The two will remain together in the same field until the harvest.

This parable describes the church throughout history, and especially those times when the church falsely inflated. The church during the time of Constantine's establishing Christianity as the religion of the Roman Empire, during the Middle Ages, and in the recent decades in America have particularly exemplified this parable of Jesus. At all of those times there were those who resembled the true followers of Christ, but didn't bear the fruit of Christ within the church.

At those times when this promised occurrence is at its height, the church is greatly weakened. This weakness continues and fosters more weakness. The church either will be choked out by the weeds or it will take a harvest event to reset faithfulness within the church.

The Reformation reset the complacent church of the Middle Ages. Worldly Christian weeds seem to have choked out the church in Europe over the past century or more. The American church stands weakened, awaiting a resolution.

The resolution that needs to occur is for a switch to flip like the one America flipped following Pearl Harbor. We went from almost zero involvement to rolling out the most incredible war machine and decisively winning the war. That intensity, energy, action, and purpose is what the church must awaken if it wants to preserve the faith of its children. Such a change could produce a radical different look for the American church. No longer would it be about facilities or programs, but American Christians would return to what Mark Batterson calls primal in his 2010 book bearing that name. The main thing would become the main thing. We would be on mission to spread the Gospel and make disciples. We would be too busy to bicker or turn from the faith. Churches would grow smaller and more intimate. Pastors wouldn't focus on growing a church but actually shepherding those who love the Lord. We would turn out soldiers for the cross as we took the training and teaching of our children and youth seriously. The fun and games would be over. Worship would become genuine.

I am afraid churches in our nation are not able to make such a change on their own. But the change will be made for us. Changes in tax-exempt status due to government regulations and an economic downturn could reduce the funds for large buildings and lavish programs. Increased religious discrimination will weed out the nominal or social Christians. We will face difficulty. We will be forced to meet in homes and smaller venues. Lack of funding and paid staff will cause us to strip down to the basics. This will be a national harvest event, but it will be for the strength of the church. The church may not be revived or reformed, but rather refined.

I don't necessarily blame pastors and church leaders for not making the needed changes or for the current weakened states of our churches. The problem is much larger. The status of American churches is the result of a cycle. Churches are a product of the society around them, and churches in return shape that society. Moral decline in churches has led to moral decline in society, and then that moral decline in society has led to further effects on the church. Now we have gotten to the point where churches are in this weakened spiritual state, but have large, expensive infrastructures and ministries that must be maintained. This creates a dilemma for church leaders who want to make a change towards faithfulness. They become a product of the system further perpetuating this cycle. The only solution is a radical change upon the church, which would actually be a refining fire.

This refining fire of the changing church landscape is happening through spiritual disasters. Already those who have not spiritually prepared have turned away. If you will spiritually prepare, then you will stay faithful when difficult changes occur for the American church, and you will be part of the refined remnant that creates a strong church that breaks the cycle. Your decision to be a spiritual prepper will impact those that come after you and are blessed by a faithful American church.

## NO COST TO ENTER

One of the reasons the American church is weak is that there is no cost to enter. Now don't misunderstand, certainly, our salvation is absolutely a free gift. Now, it was bought with a very costly price—the sacrifice of Jesus on the cross, but it's provided to us to be taken hold of at a bargain rate—free. Although salvation is free, in many places presently in the world and at many points in history there has been a high cost for someone becoming a Christian. When a Jew in Jerusalem was compelled to come to Christ and begin practicing his faith in the first century, he did so knowing he'd be banished from his family, be thrown out of the synagogue, end up in poverty, and be hunted down by Christian-killers like Saul and others. So the wheat and tares harvest was at the entrance gate, not at the end of the journey at that time. There had to be a commitment to faithfulness from the beginning. This has been true in times of intense persecution of Christians in history.

Christians today in China come to Christ knowing the activities faithfulness demands are illegal. They know they'll be risking persecution for possessing a Bible and imprisonment for witnessing to others. They know they'll have to meet in secret churches. At the onset, costs are determined for the possible believer. The commencing of one's Christian life is done knowing the dangers.

Children of Muslim families know their decision to accept Jesus as Lord and Savior will bring wrath upon them on behalf of their family and community. The certain persecution and difficulty are gatekeepers of faithfulness within church.

In America there aren't any ramifications for accepting Jesus as Lord and Savior. One can come to Christ without any idea of persecution or difficulty in mind. Actually, often it is the other extreme: they're persuaded to come to Christ with a promise of prosperity and peace. In America one has been able to decide to attend church or participate in church lackadaisically. Americans can google church names and bounce around to the church they like the best. There isn't a gatekeeper of faithfulness. Therefore, the church grows without resistance. True conversion isn't necessary because one's resolve won't be tested.

Christianity in America has enjoyed such peace and nonresistance throughout its entire history. This has created generations of American Christians who haven't been challenged in their faith.

The American church has not been forged in fire, but rather, by punch and cookies.

We've not been shaped on an anvil, but on a pillow.

## LUKEWARM AND UNAWARE

Again the seven letters to the seven churches of Asia in Revelation provide us with the greatest identification and warnings of ways in which our faith can fail. These very real, struggling churches were evaluated and assessed by Jesus Himself. Oh, how beneficial it would be to know exactly what Jesus thinks of our faithfulness. Five of the seven churches were at dangerous points. They were in danger of abandoning the faith. Three of them were especially susceptible to faith failure because of faulty foundations. There were attitudes and Christian mind-sets that put them in danger.

The most striking was the mind-set of the Laodicean church. They perceived themselves as faithful. They thought they were strong and doing God-pleasing things, but their perception was far from the truth. Their deeds made God want to vomit. He said they were neither extremely hot, like the hot springs of nearby Hierapolis, nor extremely cold, like the cold springs of nearby Colossae. Rather, they were lukewarm. They were complacent.

Reading between the lines, it appears they'd been polluted and diluted by the world. They weren't any different than the sinful world around them.

If the church made God want to vomit, then it's fair to say they were weak.

The tares far outnumbered the fruitful wheat.

The tares were choking out the wheat.

The tares were setting the church doctrines and controlling the church.

The church was so weak that they were in grave danger.

And the greatest problem was they were completely unaware of their weak state—like Samson rising to fight the Philistines after his hair had been cut. He was so complacent he didn't even realize his God-infused strength had vanished. He had no idea he was weak, so he took on the dangerous enemy and fell. (See Judges 16.)

*Complacency* may be the best word to describe the big picture of the American church. It doesn't describe every believer or every church. There are those who are very faithful, but they champion a church culture that may be as worldly as any church culture in history—rivaling the pre-Reformation church.

Like the Laodiceans, who thought they were rich and blessed by God, our American church thinks they are rich and in need of nothing, but in actuality we're not rich. Author Randy Alcorn told about a church planter in China who explained that at their church planting seminars they teach their ministry students three things: (1) Never turn down an invitation to preach. (2) Look for a place to run when you are finished preaching. (3) Be ready to die that day.[4] This church, the one that meets faithfully in secret, is the one who's rich.

## DISCOURAGED

Another fault of weak churches presented in those opening chapters of Revelation is found in the background of the sad situation in Sardis. Sardis was the dead church. They were promised that repentance could resuscitate them. Of course, there were faithful followers of Christ in Sardis. But those faithful followers were being greatly restrained by the tares within the church. The leadership of those who weren't truly saved or were living unfaithfully had quenched the power and presence of God.

Can you imagine trying to remain faithful in a dead church?

Unfortunately, you're probably very familiar with that situation. Those in Sardis seeking to be faithful and on fire had to be greatly discouraged. I'm sure they felt alone. They hoped to see God move as He had done before, but it wasn't happening. The discouragement can weigh you down.

Once we are discouraged in our church, it is easy to become disillusioned with Christianity as a whole. A dead church breeds apathy. It causes those seeking to be faithful to throw in the towel. It discourages the faithful from fighting through difficulty. Purpose and desire are lost.

This discouragement and disillusionment greatly increases our chances of turning away from the faith. Dead churches are tickets to apostasy. A high percentage of Christians striving to be faithful in America will face discouragement, since 80 to 85 percent of churches are plateaued or declining.[5]

## UNSTUDIED

Throughout high school, academics came easy for me. I'd have much rather excelled on the football field or with a guitar, but instead it was in the classroom. For my entire junior high and high school career, I was able to be exempt from every cumulative test. But in college there were no such exemptions. Since I'd studied hard for every unit test, I thought I'd remember everything for the semester final. That wasn't the case. From that point on I intensely studied for each final.

A few years later, while in seminary, I had a Greek translation test. We were told we could use the lexicon in the back of our Greek New Testaments—therefore, I didn't prepare in any way. I began taking the test and turned to the lexicon in the back only to find that my lexicon was in Spanish. I was in trouble. My test showed my lack of preparation when it was returned to me with a big red F.

The F hurt my GPA, but I lived.

What if our lack of studying could cost us in eternity?

In the seven letters, it is revealed that the churches at Ephesus, Pergamum, and Thyatira were at dangerous points due to false teachings. This reveals that a church becoming weak is in part due to a lack of knowledge of the truth. Biblical illiteracy exposes us to the onslaught of all spiritual disasters.

Currently, the American church is in one of the highest points of biblical illiteracy.

Kenneth Berding, professor of New Testament at Talbot School of Theology, has been trying to sound the alarm on America's lack of Bible knowledge. In an interview with the *Christian Post*, he said, "All the research indicates that biblical literacy in America is at an all-time low. My own experience teaching a class of new college freshman every year for the past 15 years suggests to me that, although students 15 years ago knew little about the Bible upon entering my classes, today's students on average know even less about the Bible."[6]

In his own article Berding wrote, "Christians used to be known as 'people of one book.' They memorized it, meditated on it, talked about it, and taught it to others. We don't do that anymore, and in a very real sense we're starving ourselves to death."[7]

## UNPREPARED

The American church is weak; therefore, we've been raised and are being trained in weak churches. This makes us susceptible to not surviving spiritual disasters.

Can you imagine dropping an army into a battle without them being prepared? They'd get slaughtered, yet this is happening across America with professed Christians. Children are raised in church, but when they're hit with peer pressure from high school, they snap, give in, and abandon their faith.

Students who grew up in church from birth and were once leaders in their student ministries graduate and move on to college, only to abandon the faith when their Christian doctrine is challenged by an atheist professor, or abandon their convictions to indulge in desires of their flesh.

Followers of Christ are swept out of faithful churches and denominations and join cults when they're presented with teachings that mesmerize them. Meanwhile, the remaining participants in church live out a life void of spiritual power and purpose because they're victims of the complacency around them. Soon, well-meaning followers of Christ give up from the discouragement they deal with in dead churches. Those who don't falter in their faith directly because the condition of the American church still stand on quicksand as spiritual disasters roar in the distance.

We must realize we live in a time and a nation where Christianity is near a weak point. The world has been allowed to infiltrate the church. Standards have been lowered. Complacency and apathy are rampant. We have good programs, but often we don't truly dive into the Word. We've not been warned of the possibilities of us abandoning the faith.

We must realize we're not as prepared for spiritual disasters as generations before. Our children are rendered even more vulnerable.

We must look past the status quo and prepare to stand until the end spiritually as in the heights of faithfulness in Christianity and in other parts of the world today. We can't make the mistake of the church at Laodicea and think we have it together while all the while God wants to puke watching us.

## WE CAN'T BLAME IT ALL ON THE CHURCH

Yes, we live in a time when for the most part the Western church is weak, but what should we expect when we're weak ourselves?

Looking again at the apostle Peter's spiritual disaster, we learn from the narrative that only an hour or two before he denied Christ, it was revealed that he was weak.

The night Jesus was arrested and tried, He took Peter, James, and John to pray with Him in the Garden of Gethsemane. He had them sit down and keep watch while He went deeper into the garden to pray. After praying for an hour, Jesus returned to find the three disciples sleeping. "Could you men not keep watch with me for one hour?" He asked. He went on to tell them, "Watch and pray so that you will not fall into temptation. The spirit is willing, but the flesh is weak" (Matt. 26:26–40). Jesus was aware He was soon to be arrested and crucified, and He knew the disciples would turn away and temporarily quit practicing their faith. They needed the strength and empowerment God gives when we rely on Him.

Jesus identified a difficulty we all have, which is that our flesh is feeble. Although we desire to live and serve God faithfully, we're battling our suspect flesh. Jesus was generous to His disciples in only referring to their spirits as willing because we also struggle with keeping the correct spiritual mind-set as we forget and move away from a devotion to God.

There are two aspects to what Jesus called "weak" flesh. One is the physical frailty of humans. We're mortal. We get tired. We get hurt. We die. We were created to rely on our Maker. So left to ourselves, we have limitations. Not humbling ourselves and realizing we don't solely sustain our lives leaves us at great danger of a fall. We've been warned in Proverbs 16:18 that "pride goes before destruction, a haughty spirit comes before the fall."

The other aspect is we're born dead in sin and will remain that way until we receive the salvation provided through the cross. Yet even after being made new through salvation, that "old man," our sinful nature, remains. Although the Holy Spirit equips us and empowers us for victory against our flesh, the struggle continues.

Going through life with that sinful nature presents a huge liability and the potential for being derailed by a spiritual disaster. We have to restrain our flesh, which is labor-intensive. If not "filled" with the Holy Spirit, our sin nature is a time bomb waiting to explode and shatter our faith in the process.

In our pursuit of a faithful walk with Christ, we not only deal with tendencies to forget and move away from faithfulness, but we also are just plain weak.

Before Peter's denial. Jesus had encouraged him to prepare himself. He'd asked Peter to pray with him because Jesus knew what Peter would face in the coming hours, and he knew Peter would fail.

Our flesh is weak as Peter's.

We also are extra vulnerable as Western Christians because we haven't been tested. So not only should we realize weakness exists within the church, but we need to recognize the weakness in ourselves. It's the same weakness the church in Ephesus had: they had forgotten their first love.

We, too, easily forget and turn away.

Our flesh is weak; therefore, we need to pray—we need to prepare.

## IT'S NOT GOING TO GET EASIER

The fact that in this book we moved from talking about Christians who remain faithful when faced with martyrdom to discussing those who abandoned their faith when they are excluded from certain peer circles speaks to the weakness of the American church. The struggle in America isn't going to get any easier.

My favorite baseball team is tanking this year. They've struggled to find any pitching, and their record is terrible. I listened to an interview with the coach. They recognized their struggle. They were already losing, but ahead of them were games with the best teams in the league. Something was going to have to drastically change. If they had fallen to lesser challenges, then their losing record was destined to only get worst.

With the loss of religious liberties, with increased persecution, with more difficulties in life, and with an increase in immorality, the church is only going to grow weaker. Realizing the situation is deflating. You might be saying, "if it's this bad what's the point of trying." Because that is not how God works. There is always hope. Even when destruction and ashes are certain, God always follows with a promise of bringing forth His people from the ashes. The same is true for the American church. The same is true for us, but we have to open our eyes to what is coming, and be ready. The only way we can prepare appropriately is to see the true gap of where we are and where we need to be.

Church life as we know it may implode. For the statisticians the church may look as a failure, but if we turn wholeheartedly to God and remain faithful through great challenges power will return to the American church. The power of the church in Acts will appear on our soil. Those who prepare and remain standing will experience it. Nations where Christianity is greatly opposed blaze, seem to have the strongest churches. I had the opportunity to hear a testimony of a man who helped start underground churches in Cuba during communist rule. He shared how the church exploded with growth during that time.

Heed the warnings here and set your heart on spiritually prepping; you will be excited at how much the church will be strength in the face of resistance.

# SPIRITUAL PREPPER'S CHECKLIST

Very few of us have received the preparation from our churches to equip us to remain faithful. This is why this checklist and the application of these items are imperative for our lives.

☐ Improve your Christian education and training.

Biblical illiteracy is at the forefront of the weaknesses of many churches. We need to greatly improve our educational strategy. Often the problem isn't so much with the curriculum but rather the approach and methodology. Even in the church, parents tend to put more emphasis on the child's secular education than on their biblical education. Students should be held accountable to learn and improve in their Bible studies with the same intensity and demand for excellence as they are in science, math, and English.

☐ Engage in ministry and missions.

Often the best defense is a great offense. We are called to make disciples of the world (see Matt. 28:18–20). The best thing you can do to strengthen your faith is to go on a mission trip. In my years of youth ministry, there was a direct correlation between those who went on mission trips and those who stayed faithful in their walk with Christ following high school.

# 7

# PREPPING FOR DIFFICULT TRIALS

"You will hear of wars and rumors of wars . . . Nation will rise against nation, and kingdom against kingdom. There will be famines and earthquakes in various places. . . . At that time many will turn away from the faith."

MATTHEW 24:6–10

## THE SPIRITUAL DISASTER OF A PAINFUL TRIAL IN LIFE

By her senior year everyone tried to avoid a conversation with Brandy, not because she wasn't liked or respected—it was to avoid a sermon. She was well liked, and especially respected. There was no doubt she loved Jesus, and she was sincere in her commitment to Him. Fellow students avoided her because they didn't want to hear another gospel presentation, details in Scripture she'd learned from her last Bible study, or a confrontation due to the sin in their lives that she would point out. Although Brandy was quick to give a sermon and proclaim her beliefs, she also lived out those beliefs by showing genuine love, helping those in need, and living a life of integrity.

Brandy had been faithful in her church and youth group since she trusted Jesus as her savior in the fifth grade after neighbors brought her to a vacation Bible school. She went on a mission trip each summer, worked at a summer Christian camp, mentored younger girls in Christ, and was president of the Christian club in her high school.

She was immersed in the Word and regularly spent "quiet times" with God. Her grasp of the Bible floored her student pastor. She made bold stands against some of the actions of her friends.

During her senior year she began to date Tyler. They were meant for each other—the two Christian heroes in the school had found their soul mates in each other. Tyler was the son of Brandy's pastor, and he deeply loved the Lord. He had surrendered his life the year before to student ministry. He was preparing to attend a nearby Christian college. The two practiced a godly relationship. They had built-in accountability from their youth leaders and cautiously abstained from sexual activity; they even chose not to kiss until their wedding day.

The couple went to church and Bible studies together all the time. During the summer Tyler began serving as a youth pastor. Brandy was right by his side. They worked hand in hand in the small church. They studied hard, worked part-time jobs, worked hard in the local church, devoted time to one another, and were as happy as they could be. May of their freshman year, Tyler dropped to a knee inside their favorite restaurant and gave Brandy a small diamond ring.

They were married and were devoted more than ever to their church and student ministry, and the ministry was growing.

Brandy was on cloud nine as talks of buying a house became serious. One night, Brandy was up late, searching for that dream home while Tyler was already asleep. As she scrolled through the houses on her laptop, Tyler's phone began to buzz. It buzzed once, but she didn't get up. She knew he could check the message in the morning. Then there was another buzz. Then another. Then another. Thinking it was an emergency, Brandy ran to the nightstand, picked up the phone, and at that moment her world was shattered.

It wasn't an emergency. The messages were from a girl in their student ministry. She was telling Tyler how much fun she'd had with him after school. She told him how glad she was her mom had been gone and he had come over. She went on to thank him, in much detail, for the activities they had engaged in. Brandy was crushed.

Life as Brandy knew it was gone. Her husband, her spiritual hero, had betrayed her. She'd been so devoted to God, and this was how He repaid her? God had let this happen.

Divorce followed soon—and it was "all God's fault." This was Brandy's disaster.

## THE AFTERMATH

Three years have passed, and this is the latest post on Brandy's Facebook Timeline:

Three years ago I walked away from the old Brandy. I walked away from the only "life" that I knew how to live at the time. I did not know there was anything else out there. Now three years later I realize that wasn't even the real me, and that was not "life." Now I have life, now I have freedom, and now I am my true self. There is so much fun to be had. I think I used my "devotion to God" to cover up my fear. I didn't have to step out into this amazing world, if I just blamed it on my faith.

This post was right above a picture of her at a club, with a drink in her hand. Below that was a post about how happy she was to have her boyfriend now living with her. Then there was a quote about not judging one another, with a rainbow flag draped in the background. Then the final post I noticed below that one was a picture taken of her and a group of friends at a strip joint.

The disaster struck. It was a hardship in life. In Brandy's hurt she became very angry toward God and decided her home church had forced her former religious views—views she had once held dear—on her. She states now that Christianity is a crutch for the weak and is used only so church leaders can gain power over people, and conservatives can retain political power. She also says the Bible and God's ways are antiquated. A mutual friend told me he had read a rant Brandy posted on how she had wasted her teen and college years buying into that "abstinence bull****." She now says she was a fool not to indulge in the pleasures that were available.

Brandy did graduate college and became a high school English teacher. Her boyfriend has lived with her for three months. This is the longest relationship she has had since the divorce. She tells friends she'll probably never make a complete commitment to someone again. She's dated many guys during this time and had a relationship with a couple of women. She's told one friend she still hasn't worked out who she is sexually.

A month after intercepting the texts on Tyler's phone was the last time she'd been to church. Little to no prayers have happened since. She has no idea where her Bible may be. She may have never brought it when she moved out. Basically Brandy no longer practices Christianity, thinking that is her solution. Yet in her eyes there is still hurt. There is pain. There is unhappiness. Although she has momentary fun, the joy that was once there is gone. This gives me hope and encourages me that maybe her departure from the practice of her faith is temporary. Just a phase.

Many would tell me she was never saved to begin with. You may feel the same way. It would be easy to say that; how else could someone just abandon Jesus? So I agree you'd be right to think *maybe* Brandy was never saved. If I had just heard the story and didn't know her, I could feel that way, but I was there when she made a profession of faith and walked boldly with the Lord. I saw the Holy Spirit work in her life. I believe with all my heart it was real. I also believe that's why deep down she is miserable.

Brandy's life in a tailspin. Physically she was hurt, then divorced, single again, moved, and many other things changed. When changes occur in our lives, often our spiritual life suffers.

The spiritual aftermath from this disaster in Brandy's life begins with what she's personally missed out on. The joy she had in Christ is gone. Tyler was great in her life, but he wasn't where she ultimately drew her joy. She's missing the comfort

God would be giving her in the midst of the hurt. She's missing the love and care from other Christians that she needs.

Brandy's sanctification process has been set back. She took herself off of God's proverbial potter's wheel. Her growth in Christ has been greatly stunted. Hopefully, she'll return to her first love, but when she does, she'll lament the loss of growth opportunities. Can you imagine, when Brandy is face-to-face with Jesus in heaven, the disappointment she'll feel for not having grown in Him?

She's also missing opportunities to share her faith and to serve and share God's love. The church in which Brandy served and was a member was greatly impacted by her divorce. Yes, Tyler should receive the blame, for it was his action that decimated the student ministry. It was his actions that became spiritual disasters in the lives of those students, parents, and church members. Brandy was the victim. It wasn't fair. But she still had the opportunity herself to right some of the wrong. She may have been the one person on earth who could bring healing. Instead, their church is weakened. The pastor and deacons decided not to hire another youth pastor, and the church decided it was too much trouble to keep student ministry. That decision in turn became a spiritual disaster for many within the church. Families left, and only a third of them joined another church.

Not only was the church weakened then and in the immediate future. Think of the domino effect. Those who would have been reached by their current students may never be reached. The families of those students in the student ministry may never know about Christ. It could cause a generation-after-generation departure from God. Then those in the future who could have been reached by that student ministry will not be reached. The list could go on. The aftermath can spread throughout the remaining time of earthly history. Who will not be gathered around the throne in heaven due to Brandy's departure from the faith?

Brandy reached her goal to become a teacher. She'd always dreamed of God using her in that role to make a huge impact on students, but her students each year get a much different teacher than they would have before Tyler's affair or if Brandy would turn back to Christ. And in her day-to-day life, not only is there a large number of people not being witnessed to in this aftermath, but Brandy is actually leading others away from Jesus. She now has a blog where she posts anti-Christian messages. This further encourages seekers not to seek the truth, and those out of church not to go back. Her immediate friends are being pulled into her new lifestyle. That lifestyle is in turn hardening their hearts from the tug of Christ.

## MORE DISASTERS FROM A PAINFUL TRIAL

Mandy was a devout Christian college student. She prayed and prayed for God to heal her grandfather who lay in a hospital bed, dying of cancer. Yet in a short three months he was gone. She became furious with God. How could God let her grandfather die? She'd had faith. She had prayed. She had asked. She became angry with God. She hasn't been to church since or prayed or picked up her Bible.

Angela and Corey were beyond happy as they left church following their baby son's dedication service. Their entire family had come. Yet, four months later, that same pastor who had prayed over them and their newborn and have given them a small Bible during the dedication service, was now conducting their son's funeral. He was less than a year old. The couple's hearts were broken. They immediately immersed themselves in church. Their small group wrapped the couple in love. Yet, as time went by, the couple began pulling away, and eventually told everyone they needed time. Resentment built up in their hearts against the Lord. They discontinued attending church. They quit praying. They had no clue where their Bibles were. And when they had their next two children, neither child was dedicated and neither one heard the gospel throughout their childhood.

William served four tours in Iraq. He had grown up in an atheist home, but a Christian his whole unit called "Preacher" befriended him. William saw the love of Christ personified and became a believer. He was baptized at Fort Hood. During his last tour in Iraq, he would hold Preacher's hand when Preacher went to be with the Lord. Multiple gunshots wounds did Preacher in. Walking out of the hospital, William tore the cross necklace from his neck and swore Preacher was wrong. If God would allow a good man like Preacher to die, then that God stuff was a bunch of BS.

Tom had fought through a hard life of drugs and alcohol to get his life on track. An older gentleman in a local church had been a huge influence on him. Tom was saved and baptized. He met regularly with a mentor. Tom's whole family was in church. He was beginning to get involved in an outreach ministry in the church. Then the economy took a downturn. Tom worked in construction, and new construction had completely halted. He lost his job. Then he had to file bankruptcy. Then they were kicked out of their house. Living with his wife's parents, Tom swore off all the God stuff.

Misty was so excited after fourteen years of marriage when

John finally came to church with her. It may have only been to see their daughter sing, but at least he was there. It had been raining when then left, but they had no idea the creek would rise as it did. They came home to a flooded house, and John swore he was done with God and church. Misty was heartbroken.

## DIFFICULT TRIALS IN LIFE ARE FORECASTED

Life is difficult. Hardships will arise. *Stuff* happens.

Jesus made this clear in John 16:33: "This world is *full* of trouble," He said (paraphrased). And Matthew 6:34 tells us, "*Each day* has . . . trouble of its own" (emphasis added). This is the forecasted in Scripture: there *will be* difficult trials in life. That's just part of being human.

But even worse than the actual difficulties is that those challenges can threaten our faith if we let them. Each difficulty is a fork in the road of our faithfulness.

Scripture not only warns that we'll face trials, but it also gives numerous examples of those who turned from God in the midst of those trials. When the Israelites thought Moses had died on Mount Sinai, they turned from God and created a golden calf to worship instead. When they later heard the report of giants in the promised land, they turned from God again and rebelled against Him.

The most vivid example of one turning away from God during trouble is Job's wife. When difficulty shook the couple to their core, it appears she abandoned her faith in God—and encouraged Job to do the same. In Job 2:9, after they had lost everything, she said to Job, "Are you still holding on to your integrity? Curse God and die!" How could she say such a thing?

Yet, we do. Her response to misfortune is all too common,

even among those who profess Christ. That's why Scripture warns us *not* to turn away in difficulty, because God knows we often do. There is a very real threat that Christians will turn from their faith, or at least the practice of it, in difficulty. It is a real threat for you, and for me.

But Jesus warned us that all sorts of difficulty would come. In Matthew 24 He said:

> You will hear of wars and rumors of wars, but see to it that you are not alarmed. Such things must happen, but the end is still to come. Nation will rise against nation, and kingdom against kingdom. There will be famines and earthquakes in various places. All these are the beginning of birth pains. Then you will be handed over to be persecuted and put to death, and you will be hated by all nations because of me. At that time many will turn away from the faith. (24:6–10)

Jesus' list for Christians throughout all of history, and especially for those in the last days, covered everything from civil and political unrest, to drought and starvation, to natural disasters, and even persecution. In Luke's account in Luke 21, he recorded pestilence or disease to the list. We know these things happen, but they also can destroy our faith. We, like Job's wife, naturally want to blame God and turn against Him when trouble comes. And true, He may have allowed it and not intervened, but to grow angry at God is foolish.

The trials that Jesus warned about are occurring today. They may not be the ultimate fulfillment of His prophecy, but we are seeing them, along with many other hardships. We face broken hearts, divorce, betrayal, being cheated on, family fights, health struggles, financial issues, and the list could go on, and they shake our faith. As a pastor, I have even heard individuals say that how things fall politically will determine whether or not they continue in the faith. (Yes, even the latest commentary on Fox News or CNN can be a challenge to your faith.) And things are only going to get worse. There will be more earthquakes, more natural disasters, more economic problems. Tyrannical governments will continue to arise. Sin will increase. And according to Jesus, "many will turn away," some to never return. Revelation 9:20 tells us that even after the horrific trials of the Great Tribulation, people still won't turn back to God.

So if we struggle now with difficulties, what happens when the intensity and frequency of these troubles ratchets up? What should we do?

What happens when the rumors of wars, invasions, or nuclear strikes upon the United States become more than just rumors? Will your faith still stand even when it seems God hasn't blessed America anymore?

What happens when the political scene completely unravels, and the president in the White House appears to love the enemy more than their own people? Do you keep your eyes on the Lord? Do you continue to serve Him?

In the template of the seven churches in Asia, discussed earlier, Smyrna was commended for remaining faithful when facing affliction, poverty, and slander. Though they were warned that more was coming, they were a bright light against the typical human response to difficulty. How *did* they respond to trials? They remained faithful.

We must do the same.

## YOUR FAITH THRESHOLD

The Lord has seen fit to allow me to suffer with regular kidney stones. And whatever just came to your mind to remedy them, I'm sure I've tried it. The last stone I had hit about eleven at night. My wife took me to the emergency room that night, and as she drove, I sat backwards in the passenger seat, shaking the headrest to death and screaming the whole time. The pain is so bad it turns me into the incredible hulk (minus the green skin). Miserably, we had to wait in the ER waiting room for hours, with me pacing and throwing chairs the whole time. Finally, I was taken back to the triage station and the nurse asked my pain level.

She referred me to the highly sophisticated and scientific Wong-Baker pain level chart—yes the one with smiling and not-so-smiling faces. If you've not seen one of these charts, then you're missing a good laugh. It amazes me that medical practitioners even take the chart seriously. The choices are shown on a scale from 0 to 10, with 10 being the highest amount of pain. I told the nurse I was at a 20.

The reason it amazes me that the chart is taken seriously is because we all have different pain tolerances—we all have different thresholds that make us throw chairs. My pain threshold wasn't crossed when I nearly cut my finger off with a saw or pulled my groin in a softball game, but it was when I suffered a kidney stone.

In the same way, we each have a "faith" threshold, a certain tipping point where we're tempted to throw in the towel.

But is there any problem you may face in this life that's worth throwing in the towel for eternity? Is any trial worth turning against God?

What is *your* faith threshold? Having that discussion is a

great exercise for prepping for the spiritual disaster that difficult trials can bring. I've pushed small groups within my church to have this discussion. My wife and I have personally had the discussion a few times at the dinner table. We struggle when it comes to our kids, but by talking through it, we're able to reassure one another that our faithfulness and their faithfulness to God far outweighs any difficulty we might face. This is the type of discussion Sabir and Kalila must have had in chapter 1, before they faced ISIS. It's a conversation you need to have too.

## PREPPING SPIRITUALLY FOR DIFFICULT TRIALS

Throughout this book I have used the metaphor of prepping for a *physical* doomsday to motivate you to prepare *spiritually.* In this chapter the metaphor gets fuzzy, because the two kinds of preparation collide. The physical disasters we prepare for can themselves become a spiritual disaster. Someone may build a bunker and supply it to survive a nuclear bomb. It's realistic that a nuke could be detonated. So the prepper isn't crazy, but what is he going to gain? Perhaps a few extra years in this temporal physical life. One day the prepper is still going to die.

But say a bomb was detonated and the preppers survived. They had to see their city, state, and nation ravaged. They may have lost loved ones. They may have even been harmed themselves, and because of the tragedy, they decide God is too cruel and they turn away from Him. Or they decide that if this could happen, God must not be real—therefore they turn from their faith. The eternal repercussions of one's faith are going to far exceed any extra time one may gain through physical prepping. So even when it comes to physical threats—stock market crash, home invasion, enemy invasion, flood, hurricane, or whatever it might be, though we ought to heed warnings and prep for these disasters, our faithfulness to God is far more important.

Bad things are going to happen, but don't let them turn you away from God. Instead, prepare your heart and your faith to survive them. I believe the best way to prepare is to expand your confidence in God. Expand your faith. This is what happened with Job. After losing everything, Job remained faithful, but he was teetering. Of all the things God could have revealed to Job, God revealed His own greatness and sovereignty (see Job 38 to 41). After receiving a big helping of God's greatness, Job's faith was renewed. Build up your faith now before the difficult trial of life comes.

# SPIRITUAL PREPPER'S CHECKLIST

Those who are heroes in Scripture and Christian history suffered deeply or had to step out in complete darkness and uncertainty. What stands out from their lives is faith, but that faith is also what allowed them to endure. Your confidence in God is what will bring you through spiritual disasters.

☐ Trust in God's promises.

Hebrews 11 is called the Hall of Faith. It is the who's who of God's people. All in the list accomplished great things for God, and they all held onto the promises of God when life became difficult. He has made you promises, Scripture is full of them. Everything about salvation, heaven, eternity, and Jesus' return is a promise. He also may have spoken particular promises to your heart about your own calling and life. He will keep them. He does not lie. So to survive the darkest of nights, we have to continue trusting in His promises. This requires knowing them for one. So we have to read the Bible and meditate on God's promises. Spend time in prayer so the Holy Spirit can confirm them to our heart. It would be beneficial to commit them to memory, to keep them at the forefront of our minds, so that when the time of uncertainty hits, we know the promise. Then we have to trust.

☐ Build up your faith muscle.

Like trusting in God's promises, building up your faith muscle means you can take certain measures to increase your faith. Read accounts of the heroes of faith in Scripture, and let that motivate you. Read over and over about David defeating Goliath, God parting the Red Sea, the crumpling of the walls of Jericho, and God stopping the Jordan River. Read accounts of heroes in Christian history, and see that God still works.

Take steps of faith now. When you are led in a direction take it. The more you do this, the more you see how God comes through.

# 8

# PREPPING FOR TEMPTATION

"At that time many will turn away from the faith . . . because of the increase of wickedness.

MATTHEW 24:10, 12

## THE SPIRITUAL DISASTER OF SIN

As a church elder, Victor had navigated the church through many difficult situations. He was a strong Christian witness in his city. He'd coached almost all the town's young men in baseball. He didn't only coach them in baseball, but in life. His own pastor told the congregation once that Victor touched more lives through baseball than most preachers do through church. And speaking of church, he was in church every time the doors opened, and he led a home group.

Victor and Isabella's marriage was a model to young couples.

They'd mentored many of the couples in their church. They oversaw the church's annual marriage conference. One time their denomination's magazine actually ran a story on their passion for marriage.

The couple's family appeared as perfect as their perfectly landscaped home. Victor had two beautiful teen daughters. Erica was cheerleader captain, and Julia was a standout in softball. They both excelled academically and were leaders in their church's student ministry. Everything seemed perfect for the family.

Although they seemed so perfect, Victor and Isabella's marriage was actually rocky. But due to their visibility in the church, they stuck it out, not wanting to let others down.

Even after the girls moved to college, Victor and Isabella continued to lead out in their church and community. To fill her extra time Isabella joined the praise team.

One day, the worship pastor asked the team to travel to an out-of-town conference, and Isabella agreed to go. They left Friday morning and got home around four o'clock Sunday. She didn't think anything about Victor not being home. She figured he had a meeting at church or had decided to play golf. She was amazed at how clean the house was; it was almost as if he hadn't been there that weekend. She called him but he didn't answer, so she left a message.

She ate supper alone. It was weird that Victor hadn't called her back, but she figured he'd be home soon. Around nine o'clock that night, she turned on her computer to Skype with Erica. Erica was a little late on making the call, so Isabella took the time to check her e-mail. There was an untitled message from Victor. She opened it up because it was rare for him to send an e-mail.

Victor was leaving her and was with another woman.

Twenty-six years of marriage—over, done. And a family left devastated.

Victor had moved in with a younger woman from work.

They'd been having an affair for a year. Victor had at first fought the temptation. He'd feel guilty after they slept together, and he'd seek the Lord for forgiveness and promise to break it off. But he enjoyed it.

The woman was young and beautiful. She was open to things he had never even mentioned to Isabella. A month ago he had decided that God didn't want him to be miserable. If it felt so good, then it couldn't be bad. He and Isabella were struggling anyway. The day he made that decision to leave, he heard a preacher on the radio say, "God wants you to be happy."

Victor had been faithful, he reasoned. He'd put in his time. He deserved a break. He deserved what he wanted. He'd raised his girls in church. It was *his* time now.

Isabella was devastated. The heartbreak would wreck her faith. Eventually she'd quit church and struggle with how God could let this happen.

It has been several years now. Victor and his mistress, Dayna, married following the divorce. They've since divorced as well. Dayna found out about the multiple affairs Victor had been having during their marriage.

Victor himself hasn't been back to church again except for Erica's wedding. He has thought more about church since his grandson was born, but he just can't seem to bring himself to darken the doors.

Victor was tempted. He sinned. He sinned again. And ultimately, he chose his sin over God.

Sin was a spiritual disaster for Victor.

## THE AFTERMATH

Victor's failure against the challenge of sexual temptation, his sin, and his unrepentance weren't a spiritual disaster for him alone, but for many others. The affair and divorce sent ripples throughout the church, the community, and Victor's workplace. The greatest ripples, of course, were in his own family. Isabella has still not gotten over the betrayal and the divorce. She's in counseling but has not returned to church. She's angry with God and feels that will never change. She believes that the whole church and the community see her as worthless because she couldn't satisfy her husband. She had done nothing wrong, but she feared what everyone thought. She's struggled with bouts of depression and has just become angrier.

Following the divorce, Isabella kept the house but is struggling financially because she'd always been a stay-at-home mom. Her depression has made it very difficult for her to find a job. It's completely blown up this once almost-perfect family. Of her two daughters, only Erica speaks to her dad, but at her wedding she had her grandfather walk her down the aisle.

The girls handled the situation very differently. When Erica faced this difficult trial, she turned to her faith. She was driven to seek the Lord. She's grown exponentially in her faith. She married a godly man, continues attending church, and actively serves the Lord.

Julia went the other way. She became so angry that she went off the deep end. She quit going to classes and flunked out of college. She lost her softball scholarship at the Division 1 university. She's living with her boyfriend. She hates the church and Christianity in general. Ultimately, she's angry at God.

Having godly parents is promising for a biblical foundation

in Victor's grandson's life, but at this time he isn't going to receive any spiritual support from his grandparents.

The church was greatly hit by Victor's sin. The elder board became divided on how to handle Victor's eldership, which eventually led to a church split. And after all that transpired, Victor showed no interest in repenting and returning.

The young men Victor had coached were also greatly hurt. There were some who'd dealt with the same temptations and would eventually give in because they lost hope in their mentor. Several of those young men dropped out of church from the disappointment of Victor's sin. The AAU team Victor had coached was disbanded when no one else picked up the job.

Victor's office was completely in shock. He had recently led one coworker to the Lord. This coworker was now devastated and has struggled greatly with his newfound faith. Those who did business with Victor were also let down.

This sin even shook the family tree. Victor's brother and mother swore to never speak to each other again after his mom defended Victor. A huge wedge was driven into the family.

And on top of it all, along with all the direct repercussions, there are many who will not be ministered to by Victor, Isabella, or Julia as a result of their unrepentance.

## MORE SPIRITUAL DISASTERS OF SIN

Gavin had a phenomenal gift. He had an incredible voice and could pick up any instrument and play it. He had trusted in Christ as a young boy at a church camp. Early in junior high he started a band doing covers of popular rock songs. His talent caused the band to take off. They began to have regular gigs. Then, following a mission trip in high school, his youth pastor convinced him to lead worship for the student ministry. Gavin had found his calling. A couple of months later, he was leading worship for the entire church. An evangelist who spoke at the church hired Gavin to travel with him during the summer. During that time he got the opportunity to record some of his worship songs. Things were taking off.

Four years later, Gavin is making his second stop at the liquor store this weekend. Earlier in the week he resigned from his worship leader position at a large church. This came as a shock to the church. Everything had been going so well.

Gavin gave up because he felt unworthy to led worship. Since sixth grade he'd tried to shake his struggle with pornography. But no matter how many times he repented and tried to leave it at the Lord's feet, it came back like a boomerang. The addiction had gotten so bad that he wasn't practicing his music anymore and didn't even have the desire to date.

Maybe Gavin will seek help and move past this addiction, but for now he's let his lack of self-control, sin, and guilt end his worship ministry. His embarrassment over quitting is keeping him from attending church.

Carol was a godly woman. She'd come to the Lord through her church's Sunday school as a child. She continued to grow in her faith and Christian service when she went to a private Christian high school and college. There at college she met her husband-to-be.

Once they married, they were active in church. Carol taught children's classes and volunteered in ministries for feeding the hungry. Soon the couple had children. With her husband, Carol grounded their three boys in church. She had a wonderful life.

That life changed after twenty-four years of marriage when Mike asked for a divorce. Carol remained strong in her faith and continued working in her church, praying regularly, and reading her Bible. She was an upright woman, but she was lonely. Two of her sons lived far off, and she barely saw the third. Her friends convinced her at forty-three that she was still young and needed to meet someone, so they offered to set her up on an online dating profile. Reluctantly, Carol agreed.

She was shocked at the number of responses that came in. Tons of men were interested in her!

Carol continued her faithful walk with the Lord and her church involvement, but she began to spend a lot of time on the computer and the phone, chatting with these men. It was flattering that so many were interested. But dating had changed a lot since she was a teenager. She knew she had to be careful.

As time went by, Carol discovered that these men didn't even want to go on a date; they only wanted to "hook up" with her. But Carol desired to please the Lord and was waiting until she remarried to be intimate. Eventually, many of those with whom she'd chatted began to disappear.

Months went by and none of the remaining men seemed to want to go out, but only wanted to sleep with her. She desired to do what was right, but she was still lonely. She also thought, *I have needs too.* Finally, one of the men who'd proposed coming over for a "hook-up" asked her to dinner. Deep down she knew his intentions, but she was so lonely. She thought to herself, *It's only dinner.* She soon found herself back at home with her date—and she gave in. It felt good to feel loved and wanted.

Guilt wore on Carol. She prayed for forgiveness and continued attending church. But a couple of weeks went by and soon she faced another weekend alone. But then the text came—and a short while later, she found herself in bed with another man.

This wasn't her!

She wrestled with guilt again, but then would find herself in the same situation. Eventually her heart would begin to harden. The guilt pushed her away from her quiet times and Bible reading. She began missing church. The next thing you know, this godly, virtuous woman was out of a church and in a web of repeated sexual relationships.

Tanesha was up for a promotion at work. She had been with the company for fifteen years and had jumped through every hoop they had asked her to. She was a model employee and had the most seniority in her group, so she was shocked to hear over the phone that the position was going to Brittany.

Brittany had only been with the company for a year. She and Tanesha were in the same women's ministry at church. Tanesha had actually been instrumental in getting her on board.

Tanesha was furious. She could not hide her anger and disdain while at work, but tried to at the Bible study gatherings.

Several weeks went by, and Tanesha knew she needed to lay her bitterness down before the Lord, but it wasn't fair. That was *her* position. She even told one of the ladies that she had been betrayed by Brittany. Soon Tanesha dropped out of the Bible study so she wouldn't have to face the source of her anger. But the anger and bitterness continued to weigh on her, and eventually she stopped attending church altogether.

Stephen's parents were pillars in their church. His dad was a greeter, and his mom volunteered in the children's ministry. They'd made church an important part of their life and Stephen's. When Stephen joined the student ministry they volunteered to help. They were faithful and never missed a meeting.

Stephen had always been a model student and a leader at church. He'd been a well-behaved kid, but his junior year, he made new friends on the baseball team. His new friends invited him to some parties, and he went. He became the life of the party and enjoyed it.

He began to change. He continued going to church, but was getting a total different reputation at school. He was partying, drinking, and sleeping around. One night, he even got in a little trouble with the law.

His parents met with the youth pastor and the senior pastor. Both pastors encouraged them to step in and discipline Stephen, to do what they could to change the trend in his life.

His parents knew what they should do. But they couldn't do it. They let things continue. They became enablers.

Strangely, in the midst of what was a difficult time for them, they dropped out of church. They disappeared. When their pastor called and asked them about it, they said they'd been busy, but they were running from God.

I'm sure it wasn't really even a conscious decision, but when they'd felt the Spirit's leading to discipline and help their son, they refused. Stephen would turn from the Lord and, in time, so would his parents.

"Sin" can mean sins of *commission*—the things we do—as in the stories of Victor, Gavin, and Carol; or they can be sins of omission—those things we know we should do, but don't—as with Tanesha and Stephen's parents. But in every case, it can lead to a spiritual doomsday.

## A FORECASTED DISASTER OF SIN AND MORE SIN

It's not breaking news that someone has sinned. Neither is it groundbreaking to warn you that you might succumb to temptations. After all, Romans 3:23 has made it clear—all of us have sinned.

Although we may have been saved, we will still battle temptation. All of us. And we'll all give into it sometimes. Now, that doesn't mean it should be expected that we will have an affair—NO! Victor didn't have to give in. And neither do you. But temptation can certainly lead to a disaster for our faith. Yet, the real disaster is failure to repent.

Obviously there would be consequences in Victor's life because of his affair. There would be consequences in the lives of the others whose stories were told as well. There is always an aftermath. Sin is disastrous to our witness and our influence on others, but Victor's sin—or anyone elses'—doesn't have to be a spiritual doomsday. Victor could be restored through true repentance. If he would humble himself before the Lord, he could be healed and his relationship with God restored. In time he would be able to restore relationships with his family and even be used in ministry again. But so far, he has not repented.

Unrepentance is the nail in the coffin to our faith.

Unrepentance drives us away from practicing our faith, and this is what I'm concerned with warning you about in this book.

I don't need to remind you in this chapter that the Bible warns us of sin and our struggle with it, but I do need to remind you that many prophecies in Scripture foretold that the world will become *increasingly* sinful. Of course, we know those prophecies exist, but sometimes we forget that they explain the condition of the world today.

Preachers often share from the podium their shock at how sinful American society has become. In one-on-one conversation those same preachers lament how "worldly" their congregation has become. They are surprised at the sins that are being committed by church members. Parents catch youth pastors in the hallway and share their disbelief at the rampant sinfulness within the high school. Researchers write of the astonishing decline of morality in America.

We shouldn't be surprised. Jesus said clearly that at the end of the age, just before his return, "many will turn away from the faith" and that "because of the increase of wickedness, the love of most will grow cold" (Matt. 24:10, 12). In other words, sinfulness will reach its max. It would not be the first time.

Universally, sin reached its peak just before the flood. God had had enough, so He destroyed the earth. This phenomenon occurred locally in Sodom and Gomorrah. God followed with local judgment. Even though this passage in Matthew refers to a climactic end (see 24:29–51), in the meantime it also serves to warn that in civilizations with high immorality, it will be difficult for believers to remain faithful. It makes sense that the more sin there is and the more it's accepted, the likelier it is that one would falter.

We have no idea if we're in this actual prophesied time just before the return of Christ, but we do know we're in a time of high immorality in America. We know that sinfulness has progressed over the last several decades. As time passes by, each society's level of sinfulness increases more than the previous generation's. We're on a trajectory to see more intense wickedness. So we must receive the warning that when sinfulness is rampant, we are ourselves more likely to allow sin to wreck our faith.

Luke 17 actually connects the culmination of sinfulness at the end of this age with the sinfulness before the flood and in Sodom and Gomorrah. Jesus said:

> People were eating, drinking, marrying and being given in marriage up to the day Noah entered the ark. Then the flood came and destroyed them all. It was the same in the days of Lot. People were eating and drinking, buying and selling, planting and building. But the day Lot left Sodom, fire and sulfur rained down from heaven and destroyed them all. It will be just like this on the day the Son of Man is revealed. (vv. 27–30)

The extent of this sin is prophesied in Paul's second letter to Timothy:

> But mark this: There will be terrible times in the last days. People will be lovers of themselves, lovers of money, boastful, proud, abusive, disobedient to their parents, ungrateful, unholy, without love, unforgiving, slanderous, without self-control, brutal, not lovers of the good, treacherous, rash, conceited, lovers of pleasure rather than lovers of God—having a form of godliness but denying its power. Have nothing to do with them. They are the kind who worm their way into homes and gain control over weak-willed women, who are loaded down with sins and are swayed by all kinds of evil desires, always learning but never able to acknowledge the truth. Just as Jannes and Jambres opposed Moses, so also

these men oppose the truth—men of depraved minds, who, as far as the faith is concerned, are rejected. (2 Tim. 3:1–8)

So although we're well aware that we experience temptation and can sin, we have to be warned that it's only going to get harder to live righteously. We also must remind ourselves of the cost of sin. Is fulfilling the desire of the flesh really worth it? Is it worth it in regard to eternity?

## PREPPING TO SURVIVE TEMPTATION

I am a child of the '80s, and I'm one of the biggest G.I. Joe fans. Just last year I found a complete collection of the old, small G.I. Joe action figures on eBay and tried to convince my wife how good they'd look in our home. As a kid I had all the G.I. Joe toys, comic books, VHS tapes, and underwear. I also didn't miss the cartoon on television. At the end of each episode was a PSA about safety. Each PSA ended with "Now we know!" "And knowing is half the battle."

I believe that in our prepping for a spiritual doomsday, knowing is far more than half the battle. The key to spiritual preparation is awareness. There are countless resources that tell us how to avoid falling to temptation and how to have victory in our lives. There are also resources and programs that can help us with specific sins. It is important to put a stop to sin in your life because continuing in those sins and remaining unrepentant can pull you away from practicing your faith. You could end up facing Jesus in eternity having been unfaithful to Him because you were too involved in a sin. We are living in a time where there is an intense level of sinfulness; therefore, we can easily be sucked into accepting sin in our own lives.

For example, in 2 Timothy 3, there is a strange prophecy. Verse 6 says that there will be men who will worm their way into homes and gain control over women. A peculiar statement, but could there have been a more exact foretelling of the circumstances we saw Carol face earlier in this chapter?

In America today, women aren't protected as they once were in the past. No longer do fathers and society protect the purity of women in dating. Many times there is not even a father in the home. With the rise in divorce, women are left in desperate situations raising children alone. Thus, teenage girls are often without supervision, free to text pictures of their bodies to young men. When these girls grow up, they find that their only option for "dating" is to give into the "hook-up" culture. To text pictures of their bodies. This is what dating has become. These women leave home, unmarried, and their homes are wide-open to all forms of communication—and all kinds of men. There are no gatekeepers in their lives. It becomes harder and harder for girls and women to remain pure and righteous. They fall. Then their guilt pushes them away from the practice of their faith. The same is true for men. With culture allowing so much promiscuity, it's hard for a man to live an upright life.

Sin is the ultimate spiritual disaster in that it's what separates us from God. It was for this that Jesus died on the cross. Through grace, God allows us to accept that sacrifice by faith and be forgiven once and for all for our sins. Unfortunately, we still struggle with sin daily, but 1 John 1:9 states that if we confess our sins, God forgives. Not only does He forgive, but He continues to have a relationship with us and involve us in His work. So sin doesn't have to be your spiritual disaster, but pride, guilt, or the enjoyment of sin can keep you from confessing those sins. This is something we are all in the danger of doing. It is that very thing that will ultimately cause many to abandon the practice of their faith.

Pastor and author John Piper addressed this great tragedy in a sermon for the ages at the 2007 Passion Conference in Atlanta. The message was titled "How to Deal with the Guilt of Sexual Failure for the Glory of Christ and His Global Cause."[1] *Christianity Today* ran an article referring to that message and another article Piper had written, called "Missions and Masturbation."[2] In *Christianity Today*, Piper shared the purpose behind his message and article:

> So many young people are being lost to the cause of Christ's mission because they are not taught how to deal with the guilt of sexual failure. The problem is not just how not to fail. The problem is how to deal with failure so that it doesn't sweep away your whole life into wasted mediocrity with no impact for Christ. The great tragedy is not masturbation or fornication or pornography. The tragedy is that Satan uses guilt from these failures to strip you of every radical dream you ever had or might have. In their place, he gives you a happy, safe, secure, American life of superficial pleasures, until you die in your lakeside rocking chair.[3]

Piper's message must be heard. The ultimate tragedy is not the sin (sexual or whatever) done, but rather, that we let the guilt or enjoyment of that sin destroy our faith and the practice of it.

One thing is certain from the teachings in the Bible: each one of us has sinned.

If we have placed our trust in the death and resurrection of Jesus, then He has acquitted us and we will not be eternally punished. We can enter into Heaven, but even after that salvation we will battle sin.

Whatever sin you may be struggling with right now, there are some decisions concerning it that you need to make to prevent it from being your spiritual doomsday.

First, chose Jesus over the enjoyment of that sin. Sometimes followers of Christ turn away because they simply enjoy the sin they are loving. As we have discussed, they may try to manipulate doctrines to make the sin they enjoy acceptable, but they still are choosing that act over God. Rarely do we think of it on that level. So I ask you first to ask yourself that question.

Second, if you chose Jesus, then it's time to work towards leaving the grips of that sin. Often that sin is habitual or an addiction. It's just not that easy to quit, but it can be done. God is not done with you. He loves you and wants to use you in His kingdom work. You need to first confess that sin to God, ask His forgiveness, and repent (turn away from the sin). He will forgive you.

Even though you are forgiven it may not "feel" that way. Often it helps to share your feelings with a trusted friend, pastor, or Christian counselor. Get involved in an accountability group. I have found Celebrate Recovery to be a powerful program.

The punishment for that sin has been removed. You have been forgiven. God's grace has covered you. Don't let it keep you down. Get up and pursue faithfulness.

# SPIRITUAL PREPPER'S CHECKLIST

Here are a couple more items for the master checklist.

☐ Create safeguards in your life.

> Safeguards are not a bad idea. We need them in our lives. Knowing that sin is truly appealing we need to set these walls in our lives to keep from falling into sin. If you have struggled with drunkenness, maybe you need to put the safeguard at not having a drink. If you have struggled with a temptation of an affair, then set boundaries, such as never being alone with someone of the opposite gender. If your temptation is pornography, use filters or accountability software. Place barriers in your life, but keep in mind that it's out of love for God, for what He has done for you and not as a way to achieve righteousness on your own.

☐ Get back up.

> Sin separates us from God, but it doesn't end our journey. When you have failed in any part of your walk with God, when you stumble and fall, get up. Get up off the mat, take another swing, don't quit. God is not done with you.

# 9

# PREPPING FOR FALSE TEACHING

"Watch out that no one deceives you. For many will come in my name, claiming, 'I am the Christ,' and will deceive many . . . and many false prophets will appear and deceive many people. . . At that time many will turn away from the faith.

—MATTHEW 24:4–5, 11, 10

## A SPIRITUAL DISASTER FROM FALSE TEACHING

When I began to serve at the church, Jim was already deeply entrenched in nearly every ministry. No one had a clue about all the things Jim did. Jim had a servant's heart, and would do anything that needed to be done. I was afraid to slip up and share a need because Jim would take care of it. With a glad heart, he'd do everything—clean the toilets, mow, weed, lead game time, and drive the bus. He'd always be the first one down to the altar to pray, whether for himself or with someone else.

I went on a couple of mission trips with Jim, and each morning he'd rise early and read his daily devotion. I can say with absolute conviction that Jim loved the Lord. I watched him live out his faith for five years. He'd been saved and baptized in that church ten years before.

Jim was always reading his Bible or the latest Christian living book, or listening to a sermon. He'd come sit down in my office and share what Dr. David Jeremiah had recently preached, or Adrian Rogers. Jim was very interested in doctrine. I never thought about why but would realize it later. Not only did I talk Bible with Jim, but we prayed for his lost children and other family members, and for the condition of the world. Jim had been so excited—I have no idea how many times he told me his brother was going to spend a week with him, and that they were going to travel around the state, catching up with family, and sneak in a couple of fishing trips. I prayed alongside Jim that his brother would come to church and hear the gospel.

Finally, the time came. After mowing the church property, Jim stuck his head in the office to remind me he'd be picking up his brother at the airport. Later that afternoon I heard a knock on my office door. Sure enough, it was Jim and his brother. Jim was so proud of his church and wanted to give a tour. I was in the middle of something I thought was important and didn't take the tour with them, but I wish I had. I wish I'd taken time to walk through the church with Jim and his brother because it would be the last time I saw Jim.

No, Jim didn't die, although I'm dead to him. Our entire

church and his family are considered dead to him. Jim walked away from the truth and straight into a cult. My heart breaks now knowing I was so close to Jim for so long, and yet I was unable to see this spiritual disaster coming.

I've tried and tried since to talk to him, but I have not been successful, so I don't know what all happened. What I do know I have gathered from his wife and his children. Jim's whole family—father, mother, brother, two sisters, aunts, uncles, maternal grandparents, and cousins—all belonged to what I call a cult. This "church" calls itself Christian, but it doesn't believe Jesus is the Son of God. They believe He was merely a historic man—a good man, but just human. This "church" also teaches that salvation is gained by doing good deeds, and unless you do certain deeds, then you can't get to heaven.

Jim joined this group wholeheartedly, and because his wife and kids wouldn't do the same, he abandoned them. The group he joined forbade him from talking to his family or anyone from his former church. Jim left his wife and children.

Every time I think about Jim and this situation, I'm left scratching my head. It's so hard to believe he'd turn away so quickly. It's as if he were hypnotized. Then to abandon his family and friends—in the name of religion—it's hard to swallow.

If there ever was someone in which I saw the fruit of salvation it was Jim. I can't bring myself to even doubt Jim's salvation, but he's been led astray by false teaching. I know now why Jim was so interested in doctrine; he wanted to win over his extended family from false teaching. Instead, the false teaching won over him.

## THE AFTERMATH

I hold out hope that Jim's eyes will be opened, and that he'll return to his family and the truth. So far, due to the boldness of Jim's wife, Sharon, in pursuing him, the spiritual destruction has been minimized, but just as the verdict is out on Jim, it is also still out on his family. Jim's wife still loves him and wants to be reunited. His children greatly miss him.

The worst destruction that could still come from this disaster is if Jim's wife or children follow him. Sharon has had her faith greatly suffer, and if it were not for her sheer fortitude, all three of their children would have followed in their dad's footsteps. She has fought doubt in God's existence since He had allowed this to happen. Although she continues to come to church, she no longer serves in any ministry or teaches the youth class. Therefore, those once touched by her ministry at church have suffered. For that matter, the church has been shaken. Although no one knew all that Jim contributed to the church, they still admired his heart for the Lord. Perhaps they are thinking that if he'd turn to another church, maybe they should consider it.

Jim's children—Alison, Brent, and Josh—have continued on the right track for the most part. Josh, who's grown and out of the home, never came to church much as a younger man, and has kept the same sketchy attendance. Alison had been saved and had been very faithful. She was becoming a leader within the student ministry before Jim split. She has faltered quite a bit since. We can tell she loves the Lord and is fighting to remain faithful, but she has had some bouts of partying, drinking, and bad boyfriends. Brent, the youngest, has not made a profession of faith. Jim and I had sat down with him two months before Jim disappeared. It seemed then the Holy Spirit was convicting Brent, but Jim's departure seems to have set Brent's obedience back.

There is no doubt his children are confused about truth. Jim and Sharon were building a strong biblical foundation for their children, but that's now crumbled. In a culture where the majority of children raised in church will leave after graduation, a shaky foundation isn't a promising starting point. I hate to say it, but more than likely Brent, Alison, and Josh are going to struggle to remain faithful to the Lord.

Jim had a best friend, Carl, whom he'd been witnessing to for years. Jim invited Carl every chance he could to church. The three of us went fishing once together. Carl had finally begun coming around. I've followed up with Carl a time or two, but Jim's turning away seems to have completely turned Carl off from church and God.

My prayers are that those who have been hurt by Jim can remain faithful in their walk with Christ, but another danger lies with those whom Jim is witnessing to on behalf of his new "church." Though Jim is currently under the spell of a false prophet and false teaching, I believe Jim truly is saved. Yet, those Jim witnesses to now may not have experienced a true salvation. If they're taught under Jim's new church, they'll believe they need to do certain deeds to be saved. They may never learn differently. They may die placing their hope in their works rather than in faith. Jim will be at fault. He's now becoming the false teacher and a spiritual disaster for many more people. He's leaving a trail of destruction behind him.

The damage is catastrophic, and if Jim ever makes it back to the truth, he'll never be able to hunt down all whom he's led astray. There will be a multiplication factor too. Those Jim has taught falsely are now raising their children falsely, and theoretically, generations could move far away from the truth of Scripture.

## A FORECASTED DISASTER OF FALSE TEACHING

Because false teaching and those who propagate it create such a wide path of destruction, Peter said the blackest, darkest hell is reserved for them. (See 2 Peter 2:17.) Due to the grave consequences of these doctrines, Jesus said it would be better for a false teacher to have a large millstone hung around his neck and be thrown into the depths of the sea to drown (Matt. 18:6).

There might not be any challenge to our faith that the Bible warns us more about than false teachings and the men and women who spread them. There are many variations of false teachings, where they come from, and the effects they bring. Sometimes ignorance or misinterpretation of God's Word leads to an accidental departure from the truth. Other times a person willingly embraces a teaching from a completely false religion, or even a faulty variant of Christianity. It can be Christianity—but taught falsely. It can even be an emphasis on a true teaching in Christianity, but at the expense of other doctrines that are minimized. Almost always, though, the false teaching benefits the false teacher.

Jim wasn't the first Christian to be led astray by false teaching. He is in a long line of those who have been duped. In the New Testament the apostle Paul confronted a church who'd succumbed to false teaching only twenty to thirty years after Jesus' ascension, and very shortly after the church's formation. He told them they had been "bewitched" and that they had "desert[ed]" the grace of Christ by "turning to a different gospel" (Gal. 3:1; 1:6). Paul went on to tell them that they were "foolish" and that though they had been "running a good race" someone had "cut in on" them and they were no longer obeying the truth (3:1, 3; 5:7).

To a certain degree Paul's letter to the Galatians is similar to one I want to write to my friend Jim. Paul probably planted the churches in Galatia. After he left, these churches were invaded by false teachers. The church would have had a few members that were Jewish, but the bulk were Gentiles. So these Gentiles had been taught the basics by Paul, and he'd have trained leaders to continue to lead after he left. These would've been "house" churches scattered throughout the province.

There is debate on what exactly happened in Galatia, but much can be gathered from the epistle itself. It seems a group of Jewish Christians infiltrated the churches of Galatia and taught that one could only be truly saved by following the Jewish law. Grace wasn't enough. They had to be circumcised, follow the feasts, and keep the Jewish diet. These teachings had a great effect upon the Galatian church. Those already in the church were buying into the teachings, and new converts were learning that was the true gospel.

Christianity was still in its infancy, and the teachings were already headed into left field!

According to Timothy George, author of the *New American Commentary on Galatians*, "Paul wrote his letter with the hope of winning them back from the verge of spiritual collapse and ruin."[1] Sounds as if George was describing the Galatians event as a spiritual disaster. A disaster may have been saved by Paul's letter. We're not exactly sure if the success of Paul's intervention, but history seems to indicate that it helped. Had it not, the spiritual collapse the Galatian Christians faced would have impacted the generations to follow, and the churches they planted would lead others astray by teaching salvation by works rather than faith.

False teaching pops up throughout the New Testament. The issue is addressed in three of the now-familiar letters to the seven churches of Asia in Revelation 2–3.

It is first mentioned in the letter to the church of Ephesus. Though they had been infiltrated by the Nicolaitans, they stood faithful and did not give in to the false teaching. History isn't quite clear what the teaching actually was, but its name came from one of the first deacons selected in Jerusalem—Nicholas. Legend has it that Nicholas had restrained himself from some type of sexual expression. Reports range from his refraining from sex with his wife to sharing his wife with others. Regardless of the exact situation, it's apparent he sought to refrain, but eventually gave in. So he may have begun the teaching "if it feels good, do it" because "God doesn't want you to suppress your desires." Thus, one could follow Christ, and then do whatever he or she wanted to sexually. In A Commentary on the Holy Scriptures: Revelation the authors write this was "disorderly conduct under the cloak of [Christian] liberty." They go on and write that is was also, "sexual laxity amounting to actual unchasity."

For this teaching to be accepted, there had to first be a denial of previously accepted teachings. So somehow these Nicolaitans had to give a reason why the Old Testament sexual laws, Jesus' teachings, and the teachings of the apostles were antiquated. Sounds like a familiar strategy. Although we can't share the doctrine of the Nicolaitans with absolute certainty, the letter to Pergamum shines more light on it.

The church of Pergamum, unlike the Ephesians, were giving

in to the false teachings of the Nicolaitans. In Christ's letter to this church, he seems to mention two false teachings being accepted in the church—that of the Nicolaitans teachings which were said to be like what Balaam had taught Balak to do to Israel in Numbers 22–25. At the surface it appears to be two different teachings, but many commentators believe that the reference to Balaam adds to the understanding of the Nicolaitans, that it is intended to be understood as the same false teachings. In David Aune's commentary of the passage he concludes, "The error of Balaam . . . appears to be connected with the teaching of the Nicolaitans."[2] Osborne agrees, "The best solution is to take this not as a comparison between two similar movements but as a comparison between a single movement (the Nicolaitans) and the Jewish tradition about Balaam: 'In the same way that Balaam subverted the Israelites, these false teachers are trying to subvert you.'"[3]

Even there we aren't given much, but we do know Balaam introduced Israel to a false religion that involved sexual immorality and eating food sacrificed to idols. The false god believed to be in question is Baal of Peor.

It's crude, but the name "Baal of Peor" is believed to mean "the god of the opening," in reference to sex. The worship of this false god obviously called for some of the most grotesque sexual practices, for Numbers 25:9 informs us that twenty-four thousand Israelites died for their sins.

So regardless of what the exact teachings were, they definitely displeased God in the past, they still angered him in the first century, and they would still displease him today. I say it's not important to know the exact details, but let's apply this to today. What you had in Pergamum were Gentiles who had worshipped idols before salvation by committing the sexual immorality their pagan religion called for and by eating food sacrificed to idols. They had come to Christ, but like us, they still dealt with the temptation of the flesh and the world. They were being faithful to God and were denying themselves in a very promiscuous society. They were surely being ridiculed for it as well. They also still had to deal with their own sexual desires and their former experiences. They fought against the grain to remain faithful.

Then someone within the church who wanted to free his own conscience to follow Christ and still do what he wanted sexually found out about the doctrine of Nicholas. He realized through this teaching that Christians could do both—remain right with God and live out sexual desires. So he began to teach that doctrine, also trying to bring others to his side to validate the doctrine and help the teacher deal with his own conscience regarding sexual sin. Soon people gravitated to the teaching because it allowed them to live out their desires *and* have a clear conscience.

This follows the pattern seen in prophecies that have been forgotten. Paul warned Timothy about false teachings and the crowds who love them:

> Preach the Word; be prepared in season and out of season; correct, rebuke and encourage—with great patience and careful instruction. For the time will come when men will not put up with sound doctrine. Instead, to suit their own desires, they will gather around them a great number of teachers to say what their itching ears want to hear. They will turn their ears away from the truth and turn aside to myths. (2 Tim. 4:2–4)

The Nicolaitans certainly fit Paul's description here. They promoted a false doctrine specifically so they could "suit their own desires" by carrying out the sexual practices they wanted to.

So those who both teach and accept false doctrines, now as then, do so in order to do what they want without bearing the conviction that would otherwise burden them. They would do well to remember that God flooded the earth for sins such as these (see 2 Peter 3:3–5).

By the way, keep in mind what we read in chapter 5 of this book: even though the false teachers are the ones doing the deed, behind them and their teachings is the work of demons.

So throughout the entire history of Christianity the church has been warned of false teachings. Those warnings are one of the most prolific topics in the New Testament.

The false teachings the churches of Ephesus and Pergamum dealt with allowed Christians to continue in sexual immorality so they wouldn't have to go against the grain of culture and they could carry out their own desires. New Testament theologian Gregory Beale suggests, "Perhaps part of the motivation for the teachers' attitude was the threat of economic deprivation."[4] The false teaching in the church in Thyatira may have been embraced to alleviate the persecution and suffering Christians faced in that city.

You may recall from chapter 3 that Thyatira had a strong structure of trade guilds. There was a guild for most trades, such as blacksmithing, silversmithing, pottery, and so on. To work and have income, one had to belong to one of these guilds, each of which had a patron god worshipped at feasts that involved idolatry, gluttony, and sexual orgies. New Christians wanted to follow the orthodox teachings laid forth by the apostles and wouldn't participate in these feasts. Because of this, these followers of Christ were ostracized and probably not allowed to work, which left them impoverished. Many Christians in Thyatira were out of work. Christian families struggled for survival. They also faced persecution because their lack of participation was thought to anger the gods.

A woman arose in the church claiming to have a new word from God that encouraged the Thyatira Christians to participate in idolatry and sexual immorality. Since the teachings allowed Christians to continue living out their immoral sexual desires, keep their jobs, avoid persecution, and still feel they were being faithful to God, people gravitated to it. The judgment pronounced against this "prophet" and her teachings shows how much false teaching displeases God.

These three churches encountered these dangerous doctrines only sixty years after Jesus ascended into heaven. Can you imagine the number of false teachings the church battles today, now two thousand years down the road? We not only deal with the new ones that arise when individuals try to cope with present struggles, but we also have to wade through those of the past!

### THE NICOLAITANS TODAY

The teachings of the Nicolaitans never disappeared, but have continually appeared in the church generation after generation. Today, in the United States, the doctrine of the Nicolaitans is leading churches and denominations to rewrite doctrinal statements to accommodate sexual freedom. As it was in the time of the Roman Empire, today we live in sexually charged nation.

As society has promoted the idea that everyone needs to do what makes them happy, all sexual expressions have become acceptable. Although Scripture clearly calls homosexuality sin and clearly defines marriage as between a man and a woman, many churches have changed their stances. They've done this in the name of being more "welcoming" to those who are homosexual, but also to protect the members within the church from persecution or scoffing. This is exactly what happened in Pergamum and Thyatira.

This is only one example of false teaching today, but it's a subtle attack upon our faith and can cause us to turn away.

This is an old adage that's been used often, but how do you boil a frog? The answer: very slowly. The idea is that if a frog were in a pan of water on the stove and you wanted to boil it without it jumping out, you'd have to slowly turn up the heat a little bit at a time. The increase in temperature would then be so subtle that the frog would never notice and would slowly adjust to it—until it was too late. That is what happens to us individually and the church corporately with false teaching. The philosophies of the world around us slowly evolve, and before we know it, we are changing long-standing doctrinal confessions. We must be on our guard against false teaching.

## AIN'T SEEN NOTHING YET

My friend Jim, along with many others today, are blinded to the truth. They're being "bewitched" by false teaching, and it's only going to get worse. For one, as sin increases, doctrines will be reshaped and retaught to ease everyone's consciences. As people's love of money grows, false "prophets" will find ways to get rich through teaching whatever attracts a crowd. As persecution escalates, churches will be tempted to adjust their doctrines so that they're not at odds with the culture. Losses in religious liberty will progress this more than anything.

With all of these factors multiplying the false teachings, we stand at a great risk because as we approach the end of the age, less truth will be taught, and churches are already weak in their training. Also, there is the promise that demonic activity will increase at the end. This, too, will cause more false teachings to rise because evil spirits fight with deception. Jesus spoke clearly of the coming dangers of deception:

> For then there will be great distress, unequaled from the beginning of the world until now—and never to be equaled again. If those days had not been cut short, no one would survive, but for the sake of the elect those days will be shortened. At that time if anyone says to you, "Look, here is the Christ!" or, "There he is!" do not believe it. For false Christs and false prophets will appear and perform great signs and miracles to deceive even the elect—if that were possible. See, I have told you ahead of time. So if anyone tells you, "There he is, out in the desert," do not go out; or, "Here he is, in the inner rooms," do not believe it. For as lightning that comes from the east is visible even in the west, so will be the coming of the Son of Man. (Matt. 24:21–27)

Can you picture what this might look like? Someone claiming to be the Messiah performs convincing miracles and feats. They may even fulfill some prophecies from the Bible or other religion. Their origin may be mysterious or other worldly. Many across the world become convinced. Christian leaders begin to confess that they have been wrong. They claim that this new Messiah is the real one, stating that Christianity has been a fraud this whole time.

Your head would spin. It would be easy to begin to doubt as the rug of your reality was pulled out from under you.

The apostle Paul shared more about this time in 2 Thessalonians. He called it the great deception. Read his inspired warning:

> Concerning the coming of our Lord Jesus Christ and our being gathered to him, we ask you, brothers, not to become easily unsettled or alarmed by some prophecy, report or letter supposed to have come from us, saying that the day of the Lord has already come. Don't let anyone deceive you in any way, for that day will not come until the rebellion occurs and the man of lawlessness is revealed, the man doomed to destruction. He will oppose and will exalt himself over everything that is called God or is worshiped, so that he sets himself up in God's temple, proclaiming himself to be God... The coming of the lawless one will be in accordance with the work of Satan displayed in all kinds of counterfeit miracles, signs and wonders, and in every sort of evil that deceives those who are perishing. They perish because they refused to love the truth and so be saved. For this reason God sends them a powerful delusion so that they will believe the lie (2 Thess. 2:1-4,9-11)

A great deception, a powerful delusion, counterfeit miracles, signs, and wonders these we will face. Sounds like a convincing scheme of Satan. Can you see how one might fall to this?

This passage connected the time of the appearing of the Antichrist (Man of Lawlessness) with this time of deception. In Revelation 13 we read of two beasts who are the Antichrist and the False Prophet. This foretelling warns that the False Prophet will perform miracles on behalf of the Antichrist and cause much of the world to worship Him. This is frightening when I think of how many have already been tricked by false teachings and lies. How will we ever stand against this ultimate deception?

Ultimately only the grace of God, but we can know the truth—we must know it. We must buckle the belt of truth around us tight so we can remain faithful to this spiritual disaster.

Obviously overcoming lies requires knowing the truth. This already has been stated in previous checklists, but it is critical that we learn what God has spoken to us.

☐ Study Scripture and doctrine.

We have been given a revelation of God that we can pick up and read. We have been given a book that explains the reality of this world and tells us how to live. I already have urged you to study, but I want to point out that the truth needs to be known.

Read the Bible; study it. But also study doctrine. Many people today attend a church and do not even know the full extent of what their church believes. Seek out the confessions of faith and doctrinal statements of your church, and read them thoroughly. Compare them with Scripture and know whether or not the doctrinal stance is truly biblical.

☐ Consider possible deceptions.

This chapter closed with warnings of the Great Deception that will come at the end of the age with the Antichrist. Most importantly we need to know from the Bible how the end is actually going to happen. While the best way to prepare to spot a counterfeit is to truly know the genuine article, we still ought to consider what deceptions might occur.

For example, one of my favorite prophecy authors is Joel Richardson. Joel has written extensively about the possibility of the Antichrist being Muslim. In his book *The Islamic Antichrist* he shares how the end-time scenario of Islam mirrors Christian eschatology. He expounds the possibility that the Antichrist might actually be the promised Messiah of Islam, the Mahdi. In his book *Mideast Beast* he presents a strong biblical case for this possibility.

This may or may not be how it goes down, but it is a possible damning deception. The possible existence of alien life forms is another possible deception. I believe the popularity of the show *Ancient Aliens* shows that many people are open to a deception there.

An area that is causing us to be at a great disadvantage in our spiritual prepping is political correctness. It keeps ministers from sharing that certain religions, so-called Christian groups, cults, and teachers are actually false.

# *10*

## PREPPING AGAINST SHINY THINGS

For Demas, because he loved this world, has deserted me and has gone to Thessalonica.

—2 TIMOTHY 4:10

### THE DISASTER OF MISPLACED LOVE

Jeremy loved being active. He grew up in the outdoors—baseball, football, basketball, hunting, fishing, hiking, camping, boating, skiing—you name it; if it was outdoors, he loved it.

Although playing ball and being in the outdoors kept his family busy, his parents kept Jeremy grounded; church was a priority for the family. They might spend each Saturday enjoying their favorite activity, but they'd be in church the next day.

Even after graduation and the beginning of his career, Jeremy continued to regularly attend and serve in church. When he began his own family, church remained a priority. He was an active member of his church and a family man. As in his own upbringing, Jeremy and his young family spent Saturdays doing their favorite activities, but they didn't miss a Sunday in church. He'd have loved spending more time on his hobbies, but responsibilities with his family, church, and work had limited the amount of time to enjoy it. The family would often go to the lake or spend time in the outdoors, but they were limited by their finances from doing many of the things they'd like to do. Even though they may not have taken the big vacations or had some of the toys they liked, Jeremy's children were growing in the knowledge of God. His oldest son and daughter had made professions of faith. He watched happily as they were baptized. His youngest daughter, Addison, was still young, but had begun asking questions.

His son, Daniel, was entering ninth grade, and his daughter Casey was entering seventh grade when life drastically changed. Jeremy and his family inherited his father-in-law's lucrative business. Jeremy and his wife, Melissa, went from scraping by to having tons of money and more free time.

The increase in income allowed the family to do and have things they had always wanted. Jeremy purchased a large RV, boats, and Jet Skis. They began to camp at some of the area hot spots and became regular fixtures at the lake. The family's time at church became less and less. They weren't only busy outdoors on weekends, but the kids became more and more involved in all kinds of other activities.

Jeremy's family drastically changed without them noticing. The change in lifestyle had tragic results on their spiritual lives.

It snuck up on them. They saw it as only missing a few Sundays in the spring and summer, but it gradually became almost every weekend. They fell out of almost all of church life. And it wasn't just church the family backed away from, but slowly they talked about God less and less. They prayed less and less. In time, their faith faded behind the excitement of their new activities and "toys."

Of course, they still attended church a few times a year. And when Jeremy ran into their pastor, he would say they'd just been busy and that they planned to be back soon. He wasn't lying; he meant it. When Jeremy heard of a special financial need, he made a point to give to that need online. His family clearly identified themselves as Christians, but the practice of that Christianity had waned and almost disappeared. An RV, a ski boat, a bass boat, Jet Skis, ATVs, vacations, hobbies, and activities had turned into a spiritual disaster for the family.

## THE AFTERMATH

The new toys and extra money were a welcome change to Jeremy's hardworking family. They'd been blessed. Jeremy was so happy for what he was able to provide his wife and children. They did make some great family memories—moments they'll treasure for the rest of their lives. But that's just it: those memories were only for the rest of their physical life, when there is a much larger life to come in the next age. The memory at the Grand Canyon or in Hawaii will mean little then. The photographs of the crazy skiing moments and the deep mud they drove their Side by Sides through won't mean much in eternity. Daniel's kneeboarding trophy will rust. Casey's homecoming queen crown will tarnish. Addison's equestrian jumping ribbons will be meaningless.

Six years have passed since the purchase of the RV. Spiritual debris has built up.

The worst of the spiritual aftermath is in the youngest child's life. Addison was just getting to the point where salvation was making sense, and was beginning to understand. Then she was uprooted from Sunday school, worship, the children's midweek program, vacation Bible school, and all other children's ministry events. For these past six years she's chosen the lake over church camp. She's now going into high school and has not made a profession of faith. Although there still might be time, the percentage of those who grow up in the church and accept Christ often goes down drastically at her age.

Addison basically grew up without the influence of church and Christianity in her life that her siblings had. She didn't form friendships with Christian kids, but rather, with nonbelievers. She started down a wrong path early in her life, getting involved in things that weren't good for her.

She also became involved in equestrian jumping. It was a good activity, but took her away further from the Lord. She has a rigorous schedule of practicing and competition. Her family has invested tons of money in her pursuit, so they sternly believe she must stay committed. Melissa celebrates that Addison has found her passion in life. They expect she'll receive a scholarship and maybe a chance of competing in the Olympics. Addison has made a place in the Olympics her life pursuit. God is nowhere in the picture now.

Daniel and Casey had both made professions of faith while growing up in church. They had a lot more Christian influence on their life. But now Daniel has been in college for a couple of years, and has not been to church or a campus ministry during that time. He's chosen his major without seeking the Lord's direction for his life. Things are serious with his girlfriend, and they're already talking about getting married, but doesn't bother him at all that she identifies as a Buddhist. He tells her it's good she believes in something.

Casey never really liked church and welcomed the change in life. She partied her way through high school and has gone completely wild in college. Unknown to her parents, she had an abortion her senior year of high school. She's struggled with the guilt since then. She's turned to alcohol and illicit relationships to avoid dealing with the hurt. She's far away from the Lord during this critical time in her life.

Not only did the pursuit of things and pleasure affect the spirituality of their family, but Jeremy and Melissa's departure had wider effects. Melissa used to volunteer at the church by providing snacks for the children's events. Everyone in church knew her, so her departure discouraged many and left a huge hole in the ministry. Jeremy had been a regular at church, so his departure has been discouraging for several. They both have missed the opportunities to serve and share the gospel. Although they do give to special needs, they don't regularly tithe. The ministries of the church would be strengthened if they did.

They've also led others astray. Jeremy and Melissa's life has become the envy of their friends and their neighborhood. Two couples who were close friends with them at church have followed in their footsteps. They purchased boats and now spend the weekends with Jeremy and Melissa, instead of at church. This has impacted the children of those couples as well as left larger holes in their church.

Another church family has gotten involved in the equestrian

competitions too, so they're now out of church. Jeremy and Melissa would be shocked to know those who have seen the pictures on their Facebook page and sought to mimic their lives. Jeremy's family has pulled others into the world and away from the Lord.

Three other families from church now feel fine about missing so much for their own activities because Jeremy and Melissa do it and seem to be fine.

Do you think Jeremy and Melissa will think their time at the lake was worth the eternal effects?

Are there activities, hobbies, or possessions you enjoy so much that you'd trade them for hearing Jesus say, "Well done, My good and faithful servant"? Is there any activity or event that is worth your children spending eternity in hell because they were so wrapped up in it that that they never had a chance to respond to the gospel? I guess if you can answer yes, then go ahead; that must be an awesome thing, but I hope you can see how the temporal things of this world pale in comparison to eternity.

## A FORECASTED DISASTER

The potential, disastrous pull of possessions and activities isn't only a New Testament warning, but is at the root of almost every warning in the Old Testament. The first two commandments in the Mosaic law are grave warnings against idolatry (see Ex. 20:3–4). God's people were sternly warned to not put any other god before God or to make an image of something and worship it. The prophets repeated these warnings, yet the disastrous practice of idolatry is found in almost every book of the Old Testament. Those pages reveal that Israel paid a heavy price because of their constant turning away from God and turning to idols.

Today, in the "developed world," we feel we're sophisticated and have moved past molded and carved idols. We no longer bow to statues, and wonder how someone could be so stupid to do so. Yet the craftiness of the demons who have always been behind the proliferation of idols have evolved them—idols today aren't molded and fashioned from wood, but usually are molded plastic with processors dropped in them. The modern equivalent of the Old Testament idols are things, entertainment, and status.

Best-selling author and teaching pastor of one of the largest churches in the country Kyle Idleman wrote, in his book *Gods at War*, that Israel "traded the Creator God for a god of their own creation." Then he said we do the same thing. "We replace God with statues of our own creation. A house that we constantly upgrade. A promotion that comes with a corner office. Acceptance into the fraternity or sorority. A team that wins the championship. A body that's toned and fit. We work hard at molding and creating our golden calves."[1]

Idleman went on to share that "anything at all can become an idol once it becomes a substitute for God in our lives. To describe the concept more clearly, anything that becomes the purpose of driving force of your life probably points back to idolatry of some kind."[2] With this understanding the American culture is full of idols. We have the largest pantheons in history. Macy's, Neiman Marcus, Target, Wal-Mart, Best Buy, Hibbett, the Apple Store, iTunes, and AutoTrader all have rows and rows of idols for our choosing. We can choose whichever we can afford. We'll devote our lives to them by working to have them.

Idolatry has always been a spiritual disaster for God's people, and it still is today. We shake our heads at the idolatry of Israel, and we're mesmerized by the proliferation of idolatry in the ancient world, but a forgotten prophecy in Scripture warns that the world has not seen anything yet. Even after the idolatrous ancient civilizations of Mesopotamia, Egypt, Greece, and Rome, the apostle Paul said there would be a future civilization with even more idols. He warned that the greatest idolaters in history were still to come. Idolatry has evolved some but will always exist. We keep patenting and promoting new idols.

Paul's prophecy concerning idolatry describes society at the winding down of history. It is an oft-quoted passage, but it's often forgotten in prophesy discussions. (You may remember this passage from chapter 8.) Although Paul's words perfectly capture the condition of America today, many fail to see them as an explanation of what's going on in American culture and the church. Paul warned the young pastor Timothy that people wouldn't turn from God only to worship chiseled idols, but they'd turn to materialism and pleasure. He wrote:

> Mark this: There will be terrible times in the last days. People will be lovers of themselves, lovers of money, boastful, proud, . . . without self-control, . . . lovers of pleasure rather than lovers of God—having a form of godliness but denying its power. Have nothing to do with them. (2 Tim. 3:1–5)

Paul meant exactly what he wrote—this would happen at the end of the age, but Timothy would come across it in his day as well. There's no doubt Paul in some sense was referring to the whole world—believers and unbelievers—but the language in the text seems to indicate he's essentially referring to professed Christians. Think on that: those who would turn from God and turn to pleasure were members of Timothy's congregation. They were those he was discipling. They were Paul and Timothy's ministry coworkers. We find in the next chapter of 2 Timothy that their partner in the ministry, Demas, turned from the practice of his faith and immersed himself in the world.

By saying that people would be lovers of pleasure rather than lovers of God, Paul seemed to be saying these people once professed a love for Him. But in loving pleasure they are denying the power of godliness (v. 5). If they can deny the power of God in their lives, then it would seem they've at least experienced it in some way.

Regardless of what point in history we're living in, we can fall into the trap Paul warned about.

Along with the warnings of idolatry, Scripture also warns us that the world can take hold of us. Paul further instructed Timothy to "endure hardship . . . like a good soldier of Christ Jesus. No one serving as a soldier gets involved in civilian affairs—he wants to please his commanding officer" (2 Tim. 2:3–4). The phrase "civilian affairs" would be equivalent to the world. This soldier passage is very similar to John's and James's warnings about the pull of the world:

> Do not love the world or anything in the world. If anyone loves the world, the love of the Father is not in him. For everything in the world—the cravings of sinful man, the lust of his eyes and the boasting of what he has and does—comes not from the Father but from the world. The world and its desires pass away, but the man who does the will of God lives forever. (1 John 2:15–17)

You adulterous people, don't you know that friendship with
the world is hatred toward God? Anyone who chooses to be
a friend of the world becomes an enemy of God. (James 4:4)

This world and its idols can derail our faith. These things
essentially are traps. We are living in the enemy's territory, and
he's covered the ground with these traps to destroy our faith. Due
to our sinfulness and our weaknesses, we can't resist the "cheese"
on the traps because we crave the things of this world. We're not
helped by the American church either because it's opened the
doors and brought much of the world into the church.

John Bunyan painted a perfect picture of the traps of this
world in *Pilgrim's Progress*. We looked at how Bunyan's classic
tells of Christian's journey on the narrow path to the Celestial
City. Every step of the way, an obstacle arises to pull him off
the path. This allegory is the story of our Christian walk. We
strive to live faithfully, but spiritual disasters arise and pull us
off course. All along the way Satan and his forces, Christian's
flesh, and the world stalk him constantly. One of the traps that
snags Christian and actually ends the journey for his friend is
the town Vanity Fair. Bunyan wrote:

Almost five thousand years ago there were Pilgrims walking
to the Celestial City, as [was Christian] . . . Recognizing the
path the Pilgrims took that their way to City went through
this Town of Vanity, Beelzebub, Apollyon, and Legion, with
their companions, conspired to set up a fair here. According
to their plan, all kinds of worthless things would be sold at
this fair and it would last all year long. At this fair, therefore,
are sold such merchandise as houses, lands, businesses, places,
honors, promotions, titles, countries, kingdoms, desires,

pleasures, and delights of all sorts such as prostitutes, brothels, wives, husbands, children, masters, servants, lives, blood, bodies, soul, silver, gold, pearls, precious stones, and so forth. Besides this, to be seen at all times at this fair are all kinds of juggling, cheats, games, fools, apes, rascals, and mischief makers . . . The way to Celestial City goes right through the town where this lively fair is located, and all who desire to go to the city and yet avoid going through this town "would have to leave this world."[3]

Bunyan captured the entrapping of this world with his unique metaphor.

The world we are living in is the new Vanity Fair, and we're in danger of falling in love with the things of the city and giving up our pursuit of Christ. This spiritual disaster doesn't come out of the blue; we've been warned of the danger.

## THE REALITY OF THE PULL OF SHINY THINGS

At lunch with a group of pastors, I asked them about their summer attendance—all of our worship services were down. I believe it's completely understandable because family vacations are important. I'm going to be out two to three Sundays a year doing the same thing. But after twenty years of ministry, every year the pull of the activities of the world on those in the church I have served are growing. Attendance even for the dedicated core of the congregation grows more and more irregular. National studies have revealed this as presented in chapter 1.

To help us deal with our individual discouragement, I asked the pastors around me at the table to help me construct a list of all the reasons people weren't in worship that past Sunday.

Some members had given their pastors an excuse; other members were busted by their Facebook posts. The list of reasons is mind-blowing, I had to cut it down, but it originally took four pages. It's an aerial view of Vanity Fair. People in our churches didn't worship that Sunday morning because of:

a golf, fishing, or archery tournament

a Maroon 5 concert the night before that ended late

a bridal expo in town (doors opened at 1:00 p.m., and they wanted to be first in line)

a half-marathon in a city few miles away

ladies night out the night before, to see the late showing of *Magic Mike* (this was from Facebook; be careful friending your pastor)

a dinner theater matinee beginning at noon

an air show later in the afternoon (they wanted to get a good spot)

a comic convention

a trip to the lake, the beach, or Disney World

a cruise

a gun expo

a ski trip, casino trip, or family hiking trip

a day of tubing or Jet Skiing

camping, fishing, or a canoe trip

ATV mud riding

a vocalist competition

participation in a car show

a son's wakeboard competition, trap shooting competition, baseball tournament, or 7on7 football tournament

a daughter's swim meet, softball tournament, cheerleading competition, volleyball camp, horse show, or out-of-town gymnastic competition

a work kickball tournament

a son and daughter's basketball tournament, wrestling meet, or rodeo

a husband's bowling tournament

staying up late the night before watching a UFC fight

Girl Scouts camp ending (the parents had to pick up their daughters)

that afternoon's NASCAR race (they didn't want to miss the start)

These were just the *confessed* reasons or reasons deducted from Facebook from *one* Sunday. This was only a sliver of the American reality of events on a Sunday in the summer. We live in the greatest Vanity Fair the world has ever seen. The things and events in America are a masterpiece trap customized by Satan—a culmination of six thousand years of tricking people. None of these events or things are evil in themselves. There's nothing wrong with them even stealing a Sunday or two, but these shiny things are pulling us away from our faith and the practice of it.

Just as Esau traded his birthright for a bowl of stew, we trade God for pleasure. And just as Jeremy's family were snared in this trap, so are we. We turn away from God while still having the best of intentions.

Bunyan seemed to be writing about us when he said that the city of Vanity was inhabited by those who were once journeying to the Celestial City, but the cheap trinkets and foolish entertainment had stopped them in their tracks. In the pursuit of Christ, we can begin to window-shop, and the next thing we know, we're stopping our pursuit of Him to drive a certain vehicle or wear something that caught our eyes. We get off the path of life and step onto the playground of entertainment—whether it's a theater, an iPad, a baseball diamond, a gridiron, eighteen holes, a mall, or a rocking bar—and before long time has gone by, life approaches its end, and we have given up the journey. And as I've expressed in chapter after chapter, our departure from the faith doesn't only affect us—it becomes a disaster for many. When we settle in a home in Vanity Fair in this world, our children grow up in Vanity Fair and never hear about the Celestial City. Or maybe the Celestial City doesn't sound worth their lives when *this* world has so much to offer. We hold our spouses in the world as well.

As Jeremy's family did, through their new reputation, we pull others off the path of life and sell them the crappy goods of Vanity Fair. We move from just being guilty of not sharing Christ to also becoming an agent of Satan to derail the faith of others.

Do you still doubt that materialism and entertainment can be spiritual disasters? They've been the spiritual doomsday of many.

*Right now* you and I are being pulled by this world.

Paul's prophecy in 2 Timothy is about the end of this age, but if we're not as close to the end as we think, there is no doubt the Holy Spirit was speaking of the modern world—America especially. If there is going to be another civilization, after ours, with such materialism and entertainment, we may not stand a chance. You and I are in the nation that offers the greatest opportunity to be lovers of ourselves, lovers of money, and lovers of pleasure rather than lovers of God. Therefore, it also offers the greatest opportunity to wreck our faith. And it's only going to get worse. Therefore, we must prepare. We have to ready ourselves to be like Bunyan's pilgrims when they walked through Vanity Fair: "They did not care so much as even to look at them [various "wares"]; and if they [the merchandisers] called upon them to buy, they would look upwards (signifying their trade and business was in Heaven) and put their fingers in their ears and cry, 'Turn away mine eyes from worthless things.'"[4]

There are some very shiny things in the world—fun things, but they are not worth your soul. They are not worth possessing or enjoying if they keep us from arriving into Eternity with a God pleasing life. It wouldn't hurt us turn our eyes to Heaven and put our fingers in our ears.

# SPIRITUAL PREPPER'S CHECKLIST

Another item to add to the checklist. Keeping an eternal perspective will prepare you against shiny things that vie for your attention.

☐ Look to the life ahead.

> The pilgrim, Christian, made it to through Vanity Fair, and all of his challenges for that matter because he kept his eyes on the celestial city. He looked past the momentary spiritual disaster to the ultimate reward. This is the plight of a prepper to sacrifice the now for a better future. For us, the better future is in the life to come. If we would keep our eyes fixed on that time then the things of this world grows dim. The popular financial radio host and author, Dave Ramsey, often says "live like no one else so that you can live like no one else." In the realm of finances this instruction is to suffer through a period of saving and not spending money on whatever whim that might come up. It is driving an older car while you save, but if this is done then one day the wealth gained would provide a luxurious life like no one else. This phrase captures how we should live on earth with eternity in view.
>
> The application of living like no one else in reference to activities and possessions is different for each of us. At the time I was led into the call of ministry my hope was to become a professional bass tournament angler. So I took the call of ministry to be God sharing He would bless my fishing career to become a platform to share the Gospel. But

as time went by I came to understand the call for me was to cut ties with tournament fishing. This is not the case for others. God actually allows them and maybe calls them to minister through an activity.

I have to constantly evaluate my life because I will let hobbies overrun my life. I have had to sell boats, cancel vacations, and pull the plug on the television to keep from losing focus. Like how we have different faith thresholds, we also have different levels of the amount of things that can be in our lives. It takes constant prayer and being willing to evaluate your life, and then obey when the Lord points out idols in our lives.

# 11

## PREPPING FOR HURT FEELINGS

At that time many . . . will betray and hate each other . . . because . . . the love of most [for one another] will grow cold . . . Many will turn away from the faith.

—MATTHEW 24:10, 12

### THE DISASTER OF HURT FEELINGS

Once upon a time, Mrs. Mitchell ran that small rural Baptist church. Her husband had been a longtime deacon before his passing. She was there every time the doors were open. She had her own seat—third row from the back, left side, inside aisle. It was *her* seat. It was the same in Sunday school—next to back row, outside aisle seat, right side, closest to the door. She had bragging rights at each fellowship dinner: everyone wanted a piece of her pecan pie. She was expected to add an item of new business during every business meeting. She taught the primary class during vacation Bible school. No one was to take her spot. It was Mrs. Mitchell's church.

She'd been good friends with the former pastor's wife. That pastor had served her church for twenty-four years. Then a new pastor came along.

This new pastor was dynamic. He brought in fun activities for children, youth, and families. The church transformed and was bursting at the seams, so it scrambled to expand the facilities. New members came into leadership.

The pastor continued to visit Mrs. Mitchell every couple of weeks, but the church was changing—it wasn't her church anymore. She knew it was good to reach out to the younger generation, but personally she couldn't stand it.

The church changed drastically, but the pastor soon moved away. Another pastor came, and then another. During the process Mrs. Mitchell's attendance began to wane. She was in good health. She just didn't like that things had changed. Fortunately, she bit her tongue and quietly faded to the background. By the time Brother Daniels arrived, the records showed Mrs. Mitchell as an occasional attender. The new pastor tried hard to reach out to all former members. He visited Mrs. Mitchell and thought he formed a great relationship with her. Still, she'd pop in a Sunday only every couple of months. She'd arrived early enough to grab her old seat, but the church was a different place.

One morning in his office, the pastor was looking through the church roll and recognized that Mrs. Mitchell hadn't been in the service for several weeks. He called, but no one answered.

So he went by her home. No one was there. He called her son but didn't get a response. The pastor left a message. A couple of days later, he called back. This time the son picked up and proceeded to rip the pastor apart. He told him his mother had been a longtime church member, but when she went in the hospital for a recent hip surgery, no one had checked on her. He relayed that his mother was especially upset with the pastor and was never returning to church. Mrs. Mitchell's son hung up before the pastor could get a word in.

Brother Daniels set the phone down. He was disappointed in himself. He hated to let someone down. He also hated that they'd not let him tell the truth: that he had no idea she'd had surgery. If he had known, he'd have been there.

In chapter 1, we read about a man in the Middle East who answered the door and faced five Islamic State soldiers. He knew they were there to kill him and his family if they did not deny Christianity. The soldiers asked him a question: "Are you a Christian?" Sabir remained faithful.

Mrs. Mitchell was considered the exemplary Christianity in her church and community. When she became angry at the pastor, she also faced that question, though not directly. Remaining faithful to God would not mean death for her, as it had for Sabir; it would only mean she would have to work through her anger. Yet she chose to be unfaithful. In a sense, what she was saying was that she was *not* a Christian. She abandoned her faith.

## THE AFTERMATH

The fallout from Mrs. Mitchell's pettiness had begun several years before. Despite her age she had a large network of friends. When the church began to change, she called her friends and shared her frustration over the phone. This swayed them to her side.

The church had three pastors in an eight-year span. Many of the discouraging statements made to the first of those three was due to Mrs. Mitchell's phone calls. Three deacons heavily opposed him because of her griping. The stunted business meetings were due to her dissent. A primary reason for the dynamic pastor's early moving was the opposition he faced, directly attributable to her. She'd never know the torment she put that young family through. An amazing work of God was quenched through her actions.

Three families left the church because of Mrs. Mitchell's complaining. One left because she'd complained that they were in her seat. Two others had allowed her to convince them that the pastor was unbiblical because he let the student ministry form a worship band.

Her final departure produced the greatest aftershocks. Her dissent would eventually cause church members to choose sides and crush the unity within the church. The pastor was greatly disheartened and dialed back his efforts. Mrs. Mitchell's two children and six grandchildren also ceased their involvement in the church. Her unsaved son-in-law, who had begun to attend, would quit and consequently be pushed further from the gospel. Her daughter, who was a longtime children's Sunday school teacher, quit teaching. Future students would miss out on her influence.

Mrs. Mitchell had been a strong prayer warrior, but her bitterness drove her up off her knees. There is no way to quantitate the loss of prayers, but it surely was detrimental to the ministries and people on her prayer list.

Six years have passed, and none of the family attends any

church. They've filled their weekends with other activities. Two of her grandchildren are starting families of their own, but their Christianity has been left in the dust. They've both married unbelievers, and their future children quite possibly won't grow up in church. A family with a strong spiritual heritage had fallen.

## ANOTHER DISASTER OF HURT FEELINGS

Lacy came to our church off and on. Probably every six weeks or so, she would pop in. We'd visited some, but it was hard to learn much about Lacy's life. All I knew was that her son enjoyed the youth group and that she was worried about her husband, Don, who wouldn't go to church with her. She often asked for prayer for him. I visited him several times. He was a quiet man, and it was hard to carry on much of a conversation with him.

One day Don showed up at church. I made a point to hunt him down and shake his hand. I tried again to strike up a conversation, but it was very difficult. Our church tries to be very friendly and accepting. Anyone who enters the church has to make it through three or four lines of greeters. One has to time it just right to make it in un-greeted. I sent Don a letter that Monday letting him know we were glad to have him.

Time went by, and I realized it had been some time since Lacy had been to church. Again, though, she averaged about once every six weeks, so it wasn't unusual. I called to check on her and Don, but had to leave a voicemail.

I didn't get a return call, but rather an e-mail. It's never good when a pastor gets an e-mail. Rarely is it anything positive, and so was the case with this one. It was to inform me she and her family would never return. She was mad no one had spoken to Don.

She'd spent years praying for Don, but after her feelings

were hurt, she quit church—any church—therefore ruining any chance of Don attending. She pulled her son from the student ministry, which was detrimental to his spiritual growth. Those are just the effects this disaster had on her own home. Lacy's badmouthing of me and the church also turned her brother sour toward church. There would be countless others who were never ministered to because of Lacy and her brother not practicing their faith.

## THIS ONE HITS HOME

I share these warnings of the faith-derailing spiritual disasters and their aftermath because I want you to experience the best in this life and the next. I want you to trust in Christ as your Savior and follow Him wholeheartedly each and every day of your life. I want you to stand against great odds to remain faithful to Him, and be rewarded in Heaven.

In chapter 2 I revealed my heart by sharing a letter I wish I'd written to a great friend. Carl had a strong Christian heritage in his family. He was a faithful follower of Christ and powerful witness, but right now he's not practicing his faith. I personally experience part of the fallout from his departure.

In that letter I failed to disclose the actual spiritual disaster that took Carl off his faithful path. It was hurt feelings. Not persecution or ridicule. Not a life tragedy. Hurt feelings.

The hurt feelings were legitimate. A pastor had betrayed him. And it was real betrayal, very hurtful—but not worth his faith and the faith of his family. Not worth ceasing to serve God. Not worth abandoning his walk with the Lord—not at all.

Here's his story. Carl worked a grueling job of sixty-plus hours a week of hard labor. Yet, he had volunteered in every way possible while still maintaining solid family time at home. He had also served on the elder board of his church, and was very close to the pastor. In fact, Carl did everything he could to support his pastor. He was a constant sounding board for him.

One day the pastor came to him and shared the need for an increase to his expense account. After hearing him out, Carl agreed he'd speak to the rest of the elders. The next meeting was a month away, but he immediately contacted the other elders. Some of them were concerned about whether it was feasible financially, and they all agreed it would need to go before the church.

The elders were sent a finance report before the following monthly meeting. One of the elders noticed the pastor had received some expense reimbursements above what was budgeted. So he contacted the financial secretary, who shared she had raised the expense budget because the pastor told her that Carl had cleared it. As this controversy began to grow within the church, the pastor—whom Carl thought was his friend—constantly put the blame on Carl. Then others in the church turned on my friend. It was mess.

I understand the hurt. He had a reason to be hurt.

Carl left his church but immediately began to attend another. But he and his family would only attend worship because they were gun-shy about getting involved. Again this was understandable. I supported his need to back away. A year passed. Then another. Then another, and still no involvement in a Bible study or ministry. Eventually, they began attending church only occasionally. Then it went to not attending at all, and slowly my friend was practicing his faith less and less.

As I said before, his hurt was legitimate, but not worth trading in his faith.

ONE OF MANY SPIRITUAL DISASTERS

After reading about such harsh things as false teachings, great tragedies, painful physical disasters, homes and lives destroyed by war, persecution, the inability to purchase food due to our faith, and sore temptation, it may be hard for you to take this chapter seriously. It's hard to even write about this, but the majority of those I know who are part of the 42 million who profess Christianity but don't practice their faith all tell me that the reason they left the church was because they had got their feelings hurt. This is an epidemic. I included this chapter after the others to draw emphasis to the absolute silliness of letting hurt feelings impact us in such a way.

Here are some of the things I've heard:

"We'd been out of church for a long time, but no one ever contacted us."

"I had surgery, but no one provided us with a meal, like they have everyone else."

"The choir director doesn't give me solos."

"We'd been out of a church for a long time and when we came in the door, the greeter asked if the sky was falling, since we had showed up."

"I was told I had been gaining weight."

"I wasn't recognized for being a camp chaperone."

"No one spoke to me at church."

"Too many people spoke to me."

"I carried a dish to a fellowship meal, but they didn't even serve it."

The list could go on forever. Some of the things that were done or said in that list were stupid for someone to say. I literally have a section in greeter training titled "Don't say anything stupid." There are legitimate reasons for hurt feelings, but are they worth derailing the practice of your faith?

It amazes me that in all areas of life we face words or actions that hurt our feelings but go on, yet when it comes to church and religion, we wear our emotions on our sleeves.

## WHAT JESUS HAD TO SAY

In Matthew 24, Jesus warned that Christians will betray one another and that this will cause many to turn from the faith. Yet, the epidemic that is presently occurring, for the most part, isn't even betrayal. Hurt feelings are simply the natural repercussions of *people working together*. In most cases the offenses are benign and unintentional. Yes, the words and actions may hurt, but are they really worth stopping our faithfulness?

Do you want to face Jesus in eternity and tell Him the reason you quit serving Him and obeying Him was because someone didn't like the color you painted a classroom at church? Do you want to keep your children or grandchildren away from the gospel because the church changed the Bible study times? These faith-crushing events aren't the betrayal Jesus warned about, but are small openings in which demonic forces can sneak in and grab a foothold, fulfilling their mission of pushing us away from practicing our faith. Our sin nature gravitates toward a spirit of offense because it's a way out for our weak flesh. The event itself isn't a disaster, but the festering of it and our twisting of it becomes a spiritual disaster.

To help us survive these molehills that we turn into Mount Everest, we need to recognize the things that make us susceptible to turning from our faith. Behind every possible spiritual doomsday are fiery darts from evil forces. The molehills that hurt our feelings are those fiery darts. They wound and kill our faithfulness.

Remember the gauntlet drill—where the football player runs with the ball through a line while the rest of the team tries to remove the ball. These hurtful words and actions are just part of life. We shouldn't throw our hands up and quit; instead we need to do as my coach would tell us—put your head down, push forward, and clench the ball. The "ball" in this case is our prized faith.

We also need to remember that none of us in our churches— even our pastors—have arrived spiritually. We're *all* in the process of being sanctified. We're slowly shedding off our sin and slowly taking on the likeness of Christ. This is a foreign concept to many because we typically jump into church life and ministry with the idea that we're "good to go," and we expect the same from others. But the very nature of God's sanctifying work in us should warn us that there will be disagreements and that other Christians will let us down just as we let them down. Although in many ways we have been transformed, we're not perfect yet. Hurt feelings shouldn't be something we see as abnormal; it goes with the territory. Being hurt or hurting others shouldn't be an accepted practice, of course, but we should understand and expect it because we're human. We must recognize our weakness and our tendency to let small things devastate our faith.

But in most cases those who are driven away in their faith

don't recognize what's happening. They see the offense. They see the culprit, but they don't see the big picture: that they're departing from the faith. By recognizing how small offenses can be a prowling lion, seeking to devour our faith, we can prepare for this possible spiritual doomsday. We can survive. We can face words and actions that could cause pain but continue to serve.

Of the 42 million Christian I have mentioned who are no longer in church, many of them left the church due to hurt feelings. They blame the church.

Yes, the church has failed and could do things better, but the responsibility really lies with the believer who lets such events overtake him or her.

We must be prepared. How can we let a hurt feeling drive us away from what matters most? How can we let possibly something so insignificant cost us so much? Friction and hurt feelings are part of relationships. Our toes are going to get stepped on, but no offense someone could commit against you or me should drive us to a spiritual doomsday.

# SPIRITUAL PREPPER'S CHECKLIST

This the final entry into our master checklist.

☐ See the real enemy.

In any challenge to our faith, but especially those that involve fellow Christians hurting us, we need to remember the larger war and the real enemy. The larger war is that this world and Satan's forces want us to turn from our walk with Christ. When a piercing word is said towards you, when you are done wrong, or when you have conflict within the church—there is an unseen enemy cheering. Keep the big picture in your mind and following the rest of this checklist will help you do so.

# 12

## PREPPING TO OVERCOME

These are they who have come out of the great tribulation; they have washed their robes and made them white in the blood of the Lamb.

—REVELATION 7:14

IN WRITING THIS BOOK I've wrestled with whether I am Captain Obvious or a genius. Some of the stories I have told and their analyses seem so juvenile that I've worried they would force this book into being a middle school Bible study.

Yet, I've been Captain Obvious precisely because professed Christians do *abandon the faith*. Of course persecution is a difficult challenge, and of course ridicule and exclusion cause them to turn away from their faith. Evil spiritual forces, the world, struggling churches, and our weak flesh make it difficult to remain faithful. Temptation and the resulting sins have been the downfall of the faith of many. Difficult trials, false teaching, materialism, and hurt feelings have also been stumbling blocks for numerous Christians. In all of that I haven't told you anything new. This is the obvious. You know it and you struggle with it yourself.

Now, I know me being a genius isn't a reality, but I hope I have at least helped you understand that the obvious is simply a fulfillment of Jesus' prophecy in Matthew 24. It's hard for me to attend a conference or read church growth resources and not hear warnings of epidemic proportions. Although each speaker I hear and each book I read contains a solution or two, those resources are mostly overlooking the reality of this world.

Over and over I hear about:

the decline in attendance in the American church

the decline in baptisms by most denominations

the loss of prominence of the church in America

the immorality in America

the loss of upwards of 85 percent of those who grew up within the church

And the statistic that breaks my heart and that you've read over and over again is this: that 42 *million* professed Christians are not attending church and possibly not practicing their faith.

The decline of churches and denominations have led to *changes* in church methodology—such as the seeker-friendly movement, entertainment-driven worship services, and other such transformations. Meanwhile, the nation's immorality has been blamed on Hollywood, the media, liberals, hippies, and political policies.

Those who have disappeared from church have blamed the practices of the church and the culture.

Each one of these conclusions is true to some degree. Many of the new books and messages have helped strengthen church practices in a lot of ways, but the solutions have been given even as prophecies clearly explain that those current events and statistics predicted this very thing. Ultimately that's been forgotten.

It should be obvious, but it's not. The reason churches and denominations are declining, children who grow up in church leave, and millions have already exited the church is at least the manifestation if not *the* fulfillment of Jesus' prediction that many would turn away (see Matt. 24:10).

This turning away is a tragedy.

I believe one of the reasons individuals have been swept away from the faith is that the *obvious* has not been made *obvious* in recent contemporary teaching and preaching. Those who have let one of the events discussed in this book become their spiritual doomsday didn't realize it was happening or that it even could happen.

It can. And it could happen to us. Any one of us could become part of that "many."

Though the percentage is high of those who'll be in the many, there will be a remnant. God has equipped and empowered us to remain faithful. Sure, we can be part of the *many,* but we can also be part of the faithful remnant—if we prepare ourselves to stand firm.

## ANNOYING REPETITION
Along with being Captain Obvious, I've been Ranger Repeat. I'm sure your critical mind has thought, Enough with the stories.

It's the same thing over and over again—someone is walking with God, something happens, they abandon the faith, and consequences follow. Those consequences affect the person now and transcend into eternity. The fallout affects their family and others.

Yes, the stories were very repetitious, but so is the reality of the situation. Over and over we experience the effects of these disasters and still continue to repeat them ourselves. Though we witness similar stories and their effects every day, we don't let the weight of it capture us. We don't grasp the true danger. We don't comprehend the value of our faithfulness. We also think it won't happen to us.

## SEEING OURSELVES CLEARLY

In C. S. Lewis's *The Screwtape Letters*, at one point the younger demon becomes giddy because World War II has broken out. He thinks surely this will mean the certain spiritual destruction of the human he is charged to lead astray. The older demon, Screwtape, cautions his protégé. He warns that war may not be as good for their cause as the young demon thinks:

> Consider what undesirable deaths occur in wartime. Men are killed in places where they knew they might be killed and to which they go, if they are at all of the Enemy's party, prepared. How much better for us if all humans died in costly nursing homes amid doctors who lie, nurses who lie, friends who lie, as we have trained them, promising life to the dying, encouraging the belief that sickness excuses every indulgence, and even, if our workers know their job, withholding all suggestion of a priest lest it should betray to the sick man the

true condition! And how disastrous for us is the continual remembrance of death which war enforces . . . In wartime not even a human can believe that he is going to live forever.[1]

There is so much packed into these words, but what struck me was the "doctors, . . . nurses, . . . [and] friends who lie." His intentions were to say that the "system" of this world causes us to not think we're going to die. Foolishly, although we don't articulate it, we live life as if we won't die. We perceive ourselves better than we truly are. We're too optimistic.

This is especially true with regard to our Christianity. We can be too optimistic about ourselves. We tend to think we're fine while not seeing the reality that we're slipping away from a faithful walk with God, like the family who got wrapped up with going to the lake in chapter 10. They thought they were spiritually fine and were simply just spending some time at the lake, but they weren't seeing the reality: six years had passed. The family totally missed what the absence of church and an intimate walk with God does to one's heart.

The Laodicean church in Revelation 3 thought they were just fine too. They were rich and didn't feel they needed a thing, but they really needed salve for their eyes because they weren't seeing clearly. The reality was that they were "wretched, pitiful, poor, blind and naked" (v. 17).

In being too optimistic of ourselves, we respond as Peter did when he was warned that he'd deny Christ. He said he'd *never* fall. We feel this way, but we too can fall. The Bible warns in Proverbs 16:18 that a haughty spirit, such as Peter's, comes before the fall.

The main reason I've woven the letters from Revelation 2–3

throughout this book is that we need an examination like the one Jesus gave each of them. He knew their deeds, both good and bad. It's refreshing when God knows our deeds when we've done good deeds. Sometimes we get to the point where we think no one cares. He does. He knows what we do. He knows our faithfulness even when it's tiresome.

But He also knows our bad deeds. He knows our disobedience.

For those ancient churches that were in error, Jesus' message to them was "Repent." Only then could they overcome and be victorious.

With "*many*" leaving the faith today, there is real doom and gloom ahead. We must be realistic about it. We must be heartbroken. We have to know what's going on—but we also need to know that we can overcome. *You* can overcome. You can be victorious. And just listen to what Jesus promised those who overcome:

Revelation 2:7: To him who overcomes, I will give the right to eat from the tree of life, which is in the paradise of God.

Revelation 2:10–11: Be faithful, even to the point of death, and I will give you the crown of life. . . . He who overcomes will not be hurt at all by the second death.

Revelation 2:17: To him who overcomes, I will give some of the hidden manna. I will also give him a white stone with a new name written on it, known only to him who receives it.

Revelation 2:26–28: To him who overcomes and does my will to the end, I will give authority over the nations—"He will rule them with an iron scepter; he will dash them to pieces like pottery"—just as I have received authority from my Father. I will also give him the morning star.

Revelation 3:4–5: [Those] who have not soiled their clothes . . . will walk with me, dressed in white, for they are worthy. He who overcomes will, like them, be dressed in white. I will never blot out his name from the book of life, but will acknowledge his name before my Father and his angels.

Revelation 3:12: Him who overcomes I will make a pillar in the temple of my God. Never again will he leave it. I will write on him the name of my God and the name of the city of my God, the new Jerusalem, which is coming down out of heaven from my God; and I will also write on him my new name.

Revelation 3:21: To him who overcomes, I will give the right to sit with me on my throne, just as I overcame and sat down with my Father on his throne.

The fact that Jesus made these promises to those who *do* overcome reveals that the opposite may also occur. Some might *not* overcome. But Jesus' intention is that we *do* overcome. If it weren't possible to avoid a destiny of being part of the "many" of Matthew 24:10, then Jesus would haven't said we could overcome.

But He did. And we can. We can remain faithful in persecution. We can stand strong and remain righteous when tempted. We can hang on to the truth and not be led astray by subtle false teachings. We can overcome.

## THE FAITHFUL REMNANT

The apostle John shared a spectacular scene for us in Revelation 7. Let's take a look:

> After this I looked and there before me was a great multitude that no one could count, from every nation, tribe, people and language, standing before the throne and in front of the Lamb. They were wearing white robes and were holding palm branches in their hands. And they cried out in a loud voice: "Salvation belongs to our God, who sits on the throne, and to the Lamb." All the angels were standing around the throne and around the elders and the four living creatures. They fell down on their faces before the throne and worshiped God, saying: "Amen! Praise and glory and wisdom and thanks and honor and power and strength be to our God for ever and ever. Amen!" Then one of the elders asked me, "These in white robes—who are they, and where did they come from?" I answered, "Sir, you know." And he said, "These are they who've come out of the great tribulation; they have washed their robes and made them white in the blood of the Lamb." (vv. 9–15)

During the most difficult time that will ever be, the Great Tribulation—even then some will remain faithful. And if they can do it then, we can do it now.

Jesus said that someday, some upon meeting Him will hear the words "Well done, My good and faithful servant"—don't you want to one of them?

You can.

You've been equipped and empowered to do so.

You've been given everything you need to overcome.

It's amazing that in Paul's epistles he calls his audience

"saints" or "holy ones" (see, for example, Rom. 1:7 NKJV and 1 Thess. 3:13). They were no different from us today. They'd trusted Christ as their Savior, but they still battled daily with sin and struggles. But Paul was accurate in calling them holy because the work God had begun, He'd finish. They'd been given the tools to live a holy life. We have too. Being followers of Christ, we have the Holy Spirit. Therefore, we're fully equipped and empowered to have victory and to overcome.

Throughout the Old Testament there are numerous times where Israel turned away from God when facing a spiritual disaster such as those we have discussed in this book. Yet even when the whole nation became sinful, there was always a faithful remnant. This has been true throughout Christian history. Although the majority may turn away, God always keeps a remnant. He always keeps some.

I hope you desire to be part of that remnant.

## PREP TO OVERCOME

The term *prepper* to describe a survivalist conveys only one part of the whole surviving process. But the activities of a "doomsday prepper" can be categorized by three phases. The first phase is awareness. This awareness is what sets a prepper apart from the rest of the world.

The National Geographic Channel has assembled the most popular quotes for their reality television show *Doomsday Preppers*. One of the preppers who appeared on the show, Megan, said, "I still love high heels and fashion, but I'm also thinking . . . is there anything I can conceal a weapon in?"[2] Another prepper, Jason, is quoted saying, "I keep a box of crushed glass by the door for security."[3] These quotes and others leave us scratching our heads and wondering why someone would think like that. Megan and Jason think that way because at some point they became aware of potential dangers that others haven't yet noticed.

There comes a time in the life of each prepper when he or she becomes aware of potential dangers. Sometimes those dangers are real threats and sometimes not, but either way the individual decides to prep, and then determines *how* to prep based on his or her awareness. The ultimate difference between someone who prepares to survive particular physical disasters and those who don't is the awareness. Preppers I have met have either faced personal experiences or have been able to access certain information that gave them cause to pursue preparations. I have three close friends involved in some type of prepping—all three work in careers where they are daily presented with the dangers that exist in this world.

This book is meant to raise your awareness of the spiritual disasters that lie ahead. These disasters are a threat to each one of us. So as you consider how to prep for a spiritual doomsday, you need to start with becoming aware that the dangers even exist.

The second phase is the actual prepping. Usually this consists of acquiring supplies, storing those supplies, and training. This is where action steps are taken in response to the awareness that's been gained.

Although it's sad when someone needlessly perishes because of ignorance of the reality of pending disasters, it's even more upsetting when someone who's been made aware of the danger fails to take preventative measures. These are those who actually ignore the evacuation warnings and don't take precautions even though the sirens have gone off and someone has knocked on their door.

Since you're now aware of the threats to your faithfulness, you must take action.

You must prepare.

## MASTER SPIRITUAL CHECKLIST

Throughout the book we have been building a Master Spiritual Prepper Checklist. Here is that list, sharing what you need to spiritually prepare for our spiritual doomsday.

1. Recognize there will be challenges to your faith.

2. Resolve to remain faithful not matter what you face.

3. Openly discuss the dangers to your faith with family and chruch.

4. Realize you could turn away.

5. Build accountability into your life.

6. Learn to give yourself an honest self-assessment.

7. Be tough.

8. Prioritize your fears.

9. Study Christiam martrydom.

10. Stay aware of the persecution around the world.

11. Pledge allegiance to Jesus not a church program.

12. Prioritize security in your church.

13. Think strategically in your spiritual life.

14. Be filled with the Spirit.

15. Pray.

16. Improve your Christian education and trianing.

17. Engage in ministry and missions.

18. Trust in God's promises.

19. Build up your faith muscle.

20. Create safeguards in your life.

21. Get back up.

22. Study Scripture and doctrine.

23. Consider possible deceptions.

24. Look to the life ahead.

25. See the real enemy.

You have twenty-five steps to help you prepare. Many of them are still concerning awareness. Others are specific depending on the spiritual disaster, but I believe there are two overarching preparatory measures to be taken.

Number one, we must *strengthen and develop our faith*. Because *faith* is such a familiar term, I like to say that our confidence in God must grow. Consider faith a muscle. The more "repetitions" we do and the more weight we lift, the more our faith will grow.

In the life of every biblical hero, there is a progression of growth in his or her faith. Unfortunately, we don't see the entire process in most of those men's and women's lives. Yet we are privy to much of the process in Abraham's life.

As we turn the pages of Genesis, we see Abraham's faith is regularly exercised. He fails, but his faith muscle is constantly being worked. These faith exercises all accumulate into Abraham's ultimate expression of faith in his obedience to be willing to offer Isaac as a sacrifice.

We first meet Abraham in Genesis 12, where he's instructed to leave his hometown and go to a place God would show him (v. 1). Abraham showed faith by obeying, but later we see him show just as much doubt. When faced with the challenge of a drought, instead of trusting God to provide, Abraham traveled to Egypt (v. 10). There Abraham showed his lack of confidence in God again making Sarah lie and tell Pharaoh she was Abraham's sister (vv. 11–13). Then later we see him repeat that same lack of faith (Gen. 20:2). We see his lack of faith again in his sleeping with Hagar in spite of God's promise of a child (Gen. 16).

Although Abraham failed a lot of faith tests, he also passed some tests. He continued to exercise his faith. Each time he saw God show up, his faith increased. He grew in his confidence in God.

Then came the big test. Abraham was asked to sacrifice Isaac. I believe it's safe to assume Abraham had to wrestle with this greatly, but Scripture makes clear that Abraham showed faith by rising early the next morning to be obedient. (See Genesis 22.)

In this great test of faith, Abraham revealed how much his faith muscles had grown. This is what we must do. Now *we* must exercise our faith. We must regularly trust in God. We need to turn to the Scriptures and remind ourselves constantly that our God is the real God. He's the Provider and Protector. He's the ultimate winner in the end. Our faith must grow like Abraham's faith.

The challenges you've read about throughout this book are occurring in larger volume than they ever have; they will only increase in intensity and universality. We've not seen anything yet. If believers all around us are already turning away due to these present things, then how do we stand a chance in the times that Jesus described, when "men will faint from terror" (Luke 21:26)? We must build up our faith and our confidence in God in the same way that doomsday preppers build up their stockpile of supplies. The preppers who will last and survive are the ones who have a large stockpile of the right things. The ones who survive spiritually will be those who have stockpiled strength from their faith.

Along with building up our confidence in God, we must continue to constantly *walk in the Spirit*. We have been given the Holy Spirit to live within us to be our guide. By walking with Him, in relationship with Him, we can navigate through the challenges ahead.

A prepper will quickly tell you prepping isn't only about amassing supplies or weapons. It's about being trained in how to use them. Training is invaluable for the surviving. Learning to walk in the Spirit, day by day, is our training. We can't wait for the crap to hit the fan to finally begin to learn how to walk with the Spirit; we need to be practicing now.

So first, be aware; then stock up on faith and train yourself in walking with the Spirit. One more phase remains.

After all the prepping a prepper does, there comes a time when the disaster hits and then he has to use his training and supplies. It's this use of the supplies to survive that sets the prepper apart from a hoarder.

For the spiritual prepper, there will come a time when a

spiritual disaster hits and he or she has to remain faithful or, as Paul put it, to "stand" (see Eph. 6:13–18). After putting on all of the spiritual armor that Paul wrote about in Ephesians 6—after all that "prepping"—a point will come when the armored believer must stand against the enemy and fight.

The goal is to persevere and remain faithful so that on the day you see the Lord, you will hear, "Well done!"

Spiritual disasters will come. You'll be confronted by them. You can survive, but you need to prep.

In chapter 2, I wrote a letter to a friend who had once walked faithfully with the Lord, but later turned away. I wish he'd been aware of the dangers and not become a victim. I wish he had prepped and I wish he had survived his spiritual doomsday.

Would you let this be a warning and become a spiritual prepper?

# Notes

## CHAPTER 1: PREPPING FOR PROPHETIC FULFILLMENT

1.  Johnnie Moore, *Defying ISIS: Preserving Christianity in the Place of Its Birth and in Your Own Backyard* (Nashville: W Publishing Group, 2015), 60.

2.  Steve Hale, *Truth Decay: The Erosion of Traditional Values in American Culture* (Canton, GA: Riverstone, 2006), 16.

3.  Drew Dyck, *Generation Ex-Christian: Why Young Adults Are Leaving the Faith—and How to Bring Them Back* (Chicago: Moody Publishers, 2010), 17.

4.  Bob Semietana, "As Church Plants Grow, Southern Baptists Disappear," *Gleanings*, June 12, 2015, accessed October 16, 2016, http://www.christianitytoday.com/gleanings/2015/june/southern-baptist-decline-baptism-church-plant-sbc.html.

5.  David Sanford, *If God Disappears: 9 Faith Wreckers & What to Do about Them* (Carol Stream, IL: SaltRiver, 2008), 140.

6.  Katherine T. Phan, "'Lost' Christians Greatest Crisis in American Church, Says Author," *Christian Post*, accessed October 16, 2016, http://www.christianpost.com/news/lost-christians-greatest-crisis-in-american-church-says-author-32312/.

7.  David Sanford, "Stopping America's Greatest Epidemic," If God Disappears, May 14, 1970, accessed October 16, 2016, http://ifgoddisappears.blogspot.com/2015/05/stopping-americas-greatest-epidemic.html.

8.  Michael Lipka, "What Surveys Say about Worship Attendance – and Why Some Stay Home," Pew Research Center RSS, September 13, 2013, accessed October 17, 2016, http://www.pewresearch.org/fact-tank/2013/09/13/what-surveys-say-about-worship-attendance-and-why-some-stay-home/.

9.  @barnagroup, "The State of the Church 2016 - Barna Group," Barna Group, September 15, 2016, accessed October 17, 2016, https://www.barna.com/research/state-church-2016/.

10. Richard J. Krejcir, Dr., "Statistics and Reasons for Church Decline," Church Leadership. org, accessed October 23, 2016, http://www.churchleadership.org/apps/articles/default.asp?articleid=42346&columnid=4545.

11. Stoyan Zaimov, "1 in 4 Americans Don't Believe in God; Lack of Trust in Local Churches Cited as a Reason Why Adults Are Leaving the Faith," *Christian Post*, March 25, 2015, accessed October 23, 2016, http://www.christianpost.com/news/barnas-2015-state-of-atheism-report-finds-one-in-four-americans-dont-believe-god-exists-136327/.

### CHAPTER 2: PREPPING TO BE FAITHFUL

1. Daniel Burke, "Millennials Leaving the Church in Droves, Study Finds," CNN, May 14, 2015, http://www.cnn.com/2015/05/12/living/pew-religion-study/index.html.
2. Steve McSwain, "Why Nobody Wants to Go to Church Anymore," *Huffington Post*, October 14, 2013, http://www.huffingtonpost.com/steve-mcswain/why-nobody-wants-to-go-to_b_4086016.html.
3. Office for National Statistics, "Statistical Bulletin: 2011 Census: Key Statistics for England and Wales, March 2011," http://www.ons.gov.uk/ons/rel/census/2011-census/key-statistics-for-local-authorities-in-england-and-wales/index.html.
4. Joseph Liu, "Table: Christian Population in Numbers by Country," Pew Research Centers Religion Public Life Project RSS, December 19, 2011, accessed October 17, 2016, http://www.pewforum.org/2011/12/19/table-christian-population-in-numbers-by-country/.
5. @barnagroup, "The State of the Church 2016—Barna Group," Barna Group, September 15, 2016, accessed October 17, 2016, https://www.barna.com/research/state-church-2016/.

### CHAPTER 4: PREPPING FOR MORE PERSECUTION

1. D. A. Carson, *The Gospel According to John* (Leicester, UK; Grand Rapids: Inter-Varsity Press; Eerdmans, 1991), 581.
2. Vincent Funaro. "11 Christians are Killed Every Hour, Says Irish Catholic Bishop Who Warns Persecution Has Reached 'Unprecedented' High," *Christian Post*, May 19, 2015, http://www.christianpost.com/news/11-christians-are-killed-every-hour-says-irish-catholic-bishop-who-warns-persecution-of-believers-is-at-an-unprecedented-high-139312/.
3. Monica Cantilero, "Syria Church Growing as Christian Leaders Risk Lives Amid ISIS Persecution—Pastor," *Christianity Today*, August 12, 2015, http://www.christiantoday.com/article/syria.church.growing.as.christian.leaders.risk.lives.amid.isis.persecution.pasto/61695.htm.
4. George Barna, *Revolution* (Wheaton, IL: Tyndale House Publishers, 2005), 32.
5. John F. Macarthur. *1 Corinthians*. Chicago: Moody Press, 1984, 450)
6. Osborne. *Revelation*. 129
7. Colin J. Hemer, *The Letters to the Seven Churches of Asia in Their Local Setting (Journal for the Study of the New Testament Supplement Series)* (Sheffield Academic Press, 1986), 68.

8. Osborn. *Revelation*. 130.

9. Jonah Hicap, "Christian Bakers Blast Oregon Gag Order as They Draw Huge Online Funding Support," Christian Today, July 12, 2015, http://www.christiantoday. com/article/christian.bakers.blast.oregon.gag.order.as.they.draw.huge.online.funding. support/58718.htm.

10. Cheryl K. Chumley, "Idaho City's Ordinance Tells Pastors to Marry Gays or Go to Jail," *Washington Times*, October 20, 2014, http://www.washingtontimes.com/news/2014/ oct/20/idaho-citys-ordinance-tells-pastors-to-marry-gays-/.

11. David French, "For Churches That Won't Perform Same-Sex Weddings, Insurance Begins to Look Iffy," *National Review*, July 8, 2015, http://www.nationalreview.com/ article/420928/churches-gay-marriage-insurance.

12. Albert Mohler, "Criminalizing Christianity: Sweden's Hate Speech Law," *Christian Headlines*, February 1, 2015, http://www.christianheadlines.com/columnists/al-mohler/ criminalizing-christianity-swedens-hate-speech-law-1277601.html.

13. Josh Sanburn, "Houston's Pastors Outraged after City Subpoenas Sermons over Transgender Bill," *Time*, October 17, 2014, http://time.com/3514166/houston-pastors-sermons-subpoenaed/.

14. Billy Hallowell, "'Get the Hell Out': Activist's Frank Call for Military Chaplains Who Don't Support Gay Marriage and Homosexuality," TheBlaze, July 7, 2015 http://www. theblaze.com/stories/2015/07/07/activist-calls-for-military-chaplains-who-vocally-oppose-homosexuality-in-the-armed-forces-to-quit-or-be-terminated/.

15. Todd Starnes, "Atlanta Fire Chief: I Was Fired Because of My Christian Faith," Fox News Opinion, January 7, 2015, http://www.foxnews.com/opinion/2015/01/07/atlanta-fire-chief-was-fired-because-my-christian-faith.html.

16. Todd Starnes, "Missouri State Booted Student from Counseling Program over Christian Beliefs, Says Lawsuit," Fox News Opinion, May 3, 2013, http://www.foxnews.com/ opinion/2016/05/03/missouri-state-booted-student-from-counseling-program-over-christian-beliefs-says-lawsuit.html.

17. Adam Goldman and Greg Miller, "Leader of Islamic State Used American Hostage as Sexual Slave," *Washington Post*, August 14, 2015, https://www. washingtonpost.com/world/national-security/leader-of-islamic-state-raped-american-hostage/2015/08/14/266b6bf4-42c1-11e5-846d-02792f854297_story.html.

18. "Kayla Mueller's Handwritten Letter to Family While She Was in Captivity," *Washington Post,* accessed May 18, 2016, http://apps.washingtonpost.com/g/ documents/world/kayla-muellers-handwritten-letter-to-her-family-while-she-was-in-captivity/1406/?hpid=z2.

## CHAPTER 5: PREPPING FOR FIERY DARTS

1. John Bunyan, *Pilgrim's Progress in Modern English*, rev. and upd. Edward Hazelbaker (Gainesville, FL: Bridge-Logos, 1998), 31

# NOTES

2. Ibid., 80.
3. Clive Staples Lewis, *The Screwtape Letters* (New York: HarperCollins, 2001).
4. Simon was Peter's given name.
5. James Montgomery Boice, *Ephesians: An Expositional Commentary* (Grand Rapids, MI: Ministry Resources Library, 1988), 188.

## CHAPTER 6: PREPPING IN A WEAKENED CHURCH

1. Dyck. *Generation.* 17.
2. Osborne. *Revelation.* 99.
3. David Kinnaman and Gabe Lyons, *Unchristian: What a New Generation Really Thinks about Christianity-- and Why It Matters* (Grand Rapids, MI: Baker Books, 2007), 15.
4. Randy Alcorn, "17 Countries Where Christians Are Persecuted" Eternal Perspective Ministries, December 18, 2009, , accessed October 20, 2016, http://www.epm.org/resources/2009/Dec/18/17-countries-where-christians-are-persecuted/.
5. The Malphurs Group, "The State of the American Church: Plateaued or Declining," *TMG Blog,* September 5, 2014, http://www.malphursgroup.com/state-of-the-american-church-plateaued-declining/
6. Lillian Kwon, "Biblical Illiteracy in US at Crisis Point, Says Bible Expert," *Christian Post,* June 16, 2014, http://www.christianpost.com/news/biblical-illiteracy-in-us-at-crisis-point-says-bible-expert-121626/#AVK2VhSf1C65BmCd.99
7. Kenneth Berding, "The Crisis of Biblical Illiteracy and What We Can Do about It," *Biola University Magazine,* Spring 2014, http://magazine.biola.edu/article/14-spring/the-crisis-of-biblical-illiteracy/.

## CHAPTER 8: PREPPING FOR TEMPTATION

1. John Piper, "How to Deal with the Guilt of Sexual Failure for the Glory of Christ and His Global Cause," preached at Passion Conference, Atlanta, GA, January 4, 2007, http://www.desiringgod.org/messages/how-to-deal-with-the-guilt-of-sexual-failure-for-the-glory-of-christ-and-his-global-cause.
2. John Piper, "Missions and Masturbation," Desiring God, September 10, 1984, http://www.desiringgod.org/articles/missions-and-masturbation.
3. "Missions and Masturbation," *Christianity Today*, October 30, 2007, http://www.christianitytoday.com/le/2007/october-online-only/missions-and-masturbation.html.

## CHAPTER 9: PREPPING FOR FALSE TEACHING

1. Timothy George, *Galatians, The New American Commentary* (Nashville: Broadman & Holman: 1994), 90–91.
2. David Edward Aune, *Revelation 1-5*, vol. 52A (Dallas, TX: Word Books Publisher, 1997), 185.

3. Osborne, *Revelation*, 145.
4. G.K. Beale, *The Book of Revelation: A Commentary on the Greek Text* (Grand Rapids, MI: W.B. Eerdmans, 1999), 249.


## CHAPTER 10: PREPPING AGAINST SHINY THINGS
1. Kyle Idleman, *Gods at War* (Grand Rapids: Zondervan, 2013), 25.
2. Ibid., 26.
3. John Bunyan, *Pilgrim's Progress in Modern English*, rev. and upd. Edward Hazelbaker (Gainesville, FL: Bridge-Logos, 1998), 117–18.
4. Bunyan, *Pilgrim's Progress*. 120.


## CHAPTER 12: PREPPING TO OVERCOME
1. C. S. Lewis, *The Screwtape Letters* (New York: HarperOne, 2001), 23.
2. National Geographic Channel website, accessed October 7, 2016, http://channel.nationalgeographic.com/doomsday-preppers/galleries/most-memorable-prepper-quotes/at/on-fashion-47911/.
3. Ibid., http://channel.nationalgeographic.com/doomsday-preppers/galleries/most-memorable-prepper-quotes/at/on-security-47930/.

# Scripture Index

# Index

# INDEX

## P – Q

Parker, Annise (Houston mayor), 75
Paul (apostle), 13–14, 38, 71–72, 87, 88–89, 96, 150, 162–63, 166, 167, 171, 182, 183, 189, 212–13, 219
percent
  of Americans who are regular church attenders, 17
  of children and teens raised in church who will leave by age twenty-two, 16
  of churches that are plateaued or declining, 115
  of confessing Christians who are regular church attenders, 17
persecution, number of countries where Christians are facing, 66
Peter (apostle), 4, 12, 17, 31–32, 42, 43–44, 60–62, 63, 64–65, 66, 76, 79–80, 93, 94, 98, 118, 119, 162, 209
Pew Research, 17
*Pilgrim's Progress* (Bunyan), 89–90, 92, 184–85
Piper, John, 153
promises of Jesus to those who overcome, 210–11

## R

Rainer, Thom (Lifeway president), 16
Richardson, Joel, 174
Roman Empire, 52, 77, 109, 168

## S

same-sex marriage, 73–76
Sanford, David (author, *If God Disappears*), 16–17
scoffer, defined, 44
*Screwtape Letters, The* (Lewis), 92–93, 208–9
Sheepdog Seminars, 82
Southern Baptist Convention, 16

*Spirit Filled Life, The* (Stanley), 99
spiritual disaster
  defined, 3
  list of spiritual disasters that critical Bible prophecies warn about, 32
spiritual doomsday (defined), 4
spiritual prepper checklist, 2156
Stanley, Charles, 99
Strategos International, 82
Sweet Cakes by Melissa (Oregon bakery), 74
Syria, 11, 15, 68, 78

## T

tax-exempt status of churches, 81, 110
*Tortured for Christ*, 15
*Truth Decay* (Hale), 15
turn away (defined), 4

## U

United Kingdom, total number of Christians and number of nonpracticing American Christians, compared, 27
U.S. Census Bureau, 16

## V

Vietnam War, 94
Voice of the Martyrs, 57, 81

## W – Z

Washington, George, 94
*Wild Goose Chase* (Batterson), 99
World War II, 95, 208

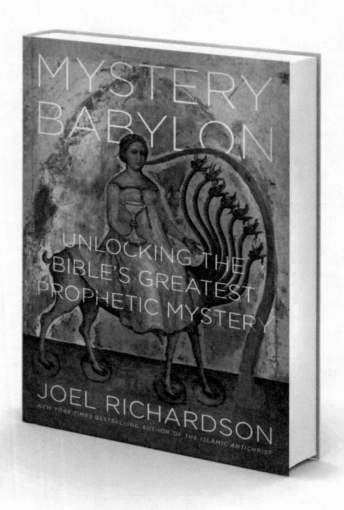

Full of practical advice on maintaining necessary medical supplies, storing food, arranging for temporary shelters and more, BE THOU PREPARED equips Christians and Christian leaders to understand the best way they can prepare themselves and their congregations so as not to be caught off guard but to be ready to help those in need when evil comes to their door.

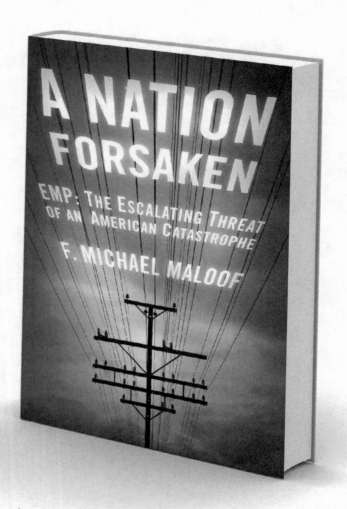

While an electromagnetic pulse event on our civilian infrastructure could be serious, it can be managed if government at the federal, state and local levels gives a high priority to undertaking preventative action to lessen its impact and enhance our ability to recover from it. Given what seems to be a perpetual gridlock in Congress, however, don't count on it.

WND Books • WASHINGTON DC • WNDBOOKS.COM

Get ready for the next emergency with SURVIVAL TIPS WITH MANNY EDWARDS. Learn about self-reliance, from vehicle preparation and tying knots to hiding your valuables and maintaining a bug-out bag. Gain the peace of mind that comes from being prepared! Manny Edwards is a lawyer, chemist and filmmaker, but most of all, a man who loves freedom. Now he works to show others how to live free and independent lives, especially in times of emergency.